Smile!
Jesus is Lord

50 MESSAGES FOR CHILDREN TO SEE AND HEAR

Lavern G. Franzen

AUGSBURG PUBLISHING HOUSE
Minneapolis, Minnesota

To Kathy and Jonathan,
To Frank and Heidi,
To Sherrie and Debbie
And to all God's little people, everywhere.

Contents

Preface

I have a very vivid memory of a certain cartoon sequence. The drawings showed a father and mother with their young son, ordering dinner in a restaurant. The first panel showed the waitress taking the order of the parents. The next drawing had her asking the child for his order. The concluding panel featured the surprised boy, saying to his parents, "How about that! She thinks I'm real."

This collection of visual messages is part of an attempt to say to the children of the church, "We think you're real! Not only that, we think you're a real part of the church as it meets to worship."

That is our theology, after all. The Christian congregation describes itself as the body of Christ, meeting in that particular place. It celebrates its unity, but it also celebrates its diversity, and claims to ignore no one as it ministers to its wide ranges of age, background, and interest. Yet we must ask ourselves if our churchly practice has been consistent with our theology. We might just find a degree of disparity we'd prefer not to admit, especially when it comes to the younger saints and sinners, the less mature parts of the body.

In saying that, we're also admitting that we may not always give our younger Christians the impression that we think they are real. Most of the time, their church life consists of Sunday morning periods of quiet sitting, broken only by the admonition of their parents or the standing or kneeling action of the congregation. And much of this focuses on what to a child are unintelligible prayers or unattractive hymns. These are directed mainly by adults, from adults, or to adults. No wonder it's hard to convince a child that he's really part of it, when his experiences seem to indicate otherwise.

These messages are designed for use in the worship life of the congregation as well as in other activities in which young people come together. They are intended to relate to children with their thoughts and their words, through their visual experiences. Through them we are inviting these young Christians into the reality of life in the Word.

For that reason, these messages are intended to be more than simple object lessons or morality play periods. The purpose of preaching to adults, and to children, is to proclaim the Good News of God's great acts for us in Jesus Christ. These messages diagnose our condition, and then share Jesus Christ as God's answer for it. Actually, each of these messages is a simplified visual presentation of that same proclamation of law and gospel for grown-ups, and can be expanded to provide adult message material. The basic problems are the same; only the symptoms change with age.

Finally, a word of thanks to the people, especially the little people, of Our Redeemer congregation whose interest and encouragement has produced these messages. I would be remiss if I did not also thank my wife, Mary Ann, for her comments and constructive suggestions. A further word of thanks to Ms. Joyce Boettger for the painstaking typing she did of this manuscript. And with them all, a word of prayer that the little people of the church might respond to all who use these words with their own thought "How about that! They think we're real."

Jesus Is Lord

SCRIPTURE

Therefore God has highly exalted him and bestowed on him the name which is above every name, that at the name of Jesus every knee should bow, in heaven and on earth and under the earth, and every tongue confess that Jesus Christ is Lord, to the glory of God the Father.

Philippians 2:9-11 (Easter)

PREPARATION

Cut four pieces of light cardboard, approximately 4" by 16" each. *(File folder material is an ideal weight for this purpose.)* On card number 1, place the words JESUS IS LORD! and the word ALLELUIA on the reverse side. Divide cards 2, 3, and 4 into approximately 4" sections for purposes of folding. Fold each card so that a 4" x 8" section appears to the front as if it were a single card, with section one and section four meeting to form that card. *(The two center sections will be hidden from view when the card is folded in this way.)* On the 4" x 8" section which appears for card number two, print the words I'M AFRAID OF THE DARK. Unfold the card and in the 8" section in the center print JESUS IS LORD! Across the entire back, print the word ALLELUIA! Follow the same process with card 3, printing the words SOMETIMES I'M LONELY on the 4" x 8" section which appears and again JESUS IS LORD! on the hidden section, with ALLELUIA on the reverse. For card number 4, print the words SOME DAY I WILL DIE on the 4" x 8" section which will appear, JESUS IS LORD! in the inner section and ALLELUIA! on the reverse. *(When showing cards two, three, and four, keep JESUS IS LORD! and ALLELUIA hidden from view at first.)*

This is an exciting day, isn't it? So many wonderful things have happened already. Some of you probably have new clothes for today. Or, many of you probably had a lot of candy this morning. I suppose you probably have quite a few Easter eggs too, right? It really is an exciting day.

But that's only part of the excitement. Really, it's not even the most exciting thing today. What do you think that might be? What are we celebrating today? *(Wait for the children to answer. If they need prompting do so, but elicit the response "Jesus rose".)*

That's right! Today is the day Jesus came out of the grave. He was stronger even than death! So we can say this. *(Hold up the card saying JESUS IS LORD.)* Let's say it together. *(Show the words JESUS IS LORD and wait for the children to respond.)* And we can say this. *(Show the reverse side with the word ALLELUIA!; again wait for the children to respond. You may wish to turn the card over and over several times, with the children responding each time.)* It really is an exciting day when Jesus is Lord *(Show card.)* and we can say Alleluia. *(Show card.)*

Of course there are some days which are not quite so exciting. For example, *(Show card number two, speaking slowly as you do.)* there are times when we are afraid of the dark. But those are not exciting times, at all. But *(open the card to show the words JESUS IS LORD!)*, we know that Jesus is Lord and he's Lord of the dark, too. So we can say *(turn the card over and allow the children to respond)* Alleluia!

Or, *(show card number three)* sometimes we are lonely and that's not exciting either But *(open the card)* we know Jesus is Lord! We know he's with us and we can say Alleluia. *(Turn the card to show it.)*

Of course, it's hard to be happy when we think that some day *(slowly show the final card)* we will die. That's really the saddest time of all. That is, it would be if we didn't have Easter. But Easter means *(open the card to show JESUS IS LORD!)* Jesus is Lord. He's Lord over death too. We can even say Alleluia! *(Show the card as you say the word.)*

That's the good news we have today. Jesus is Lord, Lord over everything, Lord over our sins, Lord over the darkness, even Lord over dying. Let's say it together. *(Show the card JESUS IS LORD and wait for the response. Then show the card ALLELUIA!)*

From Frowns to Happy Faces

SCRIPTURE

On the evening of that day, the first day of the week, the doors being shut where the disciples were, for fear of the Jews, Jesus came and stood among them and said to them, "Peace be with you." When he had said this, he showed them his hands and his side. Then the disciples were glad when they saw the Lord. Jesus said to them again, "Peace be with you. As the Father has sent me, even so I send you."

John 20:19-21

PREPARATION

Cut a file folder into thirds, to form three separate folders.

Folder No. 1: The cover should have a smiling face. Across the whole center, pages 2 and 3, JESUS IS LORD and page 4 the word ALLELUIA.

Folder 2: The cover of this folder should have a frowning face of the same size as the smiling face in folder 1. Page 2 has the words JESUS IS LORD, but; page 3, IT DOESN'T MAKE ANY DIFFERENCE; and page 4, a frowning face.

Folder 3: This cover should have a frowning face, again the same size as the others. Page 2 text reads JESUS IS LORD . . . and; page 3, HE LOVES US, HE HEARS US, HE IS WITH US, and page 4, a smiling face.

When we came to church on Easter most of us were very happy people. We probably looked just like this young man, *(show the cover of folder number one).* And we had a good reason for smiling. *(Open the folder to show the words JESUS IS LORD and wait for the children to respond. Then show page four, the word ALLE-LUIA, and again wait for the children to respond.)* That's right. Last Sunday was a happy day because we could say "Jesus Is Lord" and "Alleluia."

Of course we don't always feel quite that happy. It was very easy to say Alleluia when there was so much joy and excitement. But sometimes that joy disappears and then we begin to wonder is it really that exciting? We begin to feel more like the young man on this card. *(Show folder number two, with the frowning face.)* You see he's ready to say "Jesus is Lord" *(show the second page)*, but *(show page 3 and wait for the children to read it together),* he's not sure it makes any difference. He's like Thomas was after the first Easter.

So we can understand his unhappy face. *(Show the cover of folder number three.)* But let's see what's inside this one. *(Show pages two and three and wait for the children to read.)* That's right! Jesus is Lord and he loves us, he hears us, and he is with us.

That's the difference. Jesus is Lord and he loves every one of us. *(Point to the words for emphasis.)* Jesus is Lord and he hears us; he even told us to pray to him. That makes a difference too. Jesus is Lord and he is with us. He is with us right now as we read his word and as we receive him in the sacrament. Jesus is Lord and he makes a difference.

That's good news and that's why we can be people like this. *(Show the last page of folder 3.)* That's right, happy people. We can say Jesus is Lord *(show the inside of Folder 1)* and we know that every day of our life we can say *(show the last page and cover of folder 1)* Alleluia.

Our Country

SCRIPTURE

Then the Lord appeared to Solomon in the night and said
to him: "I have heard your prayer, and have chosen this place
for myself as a house of sacrifice. When I shut up the heavens
so that there is no rain, or command the locust to devour the
land, or send pestilence among my people, if my people who
are called by my name humble themselves, and pray and seek
my face, and turn from their wicked ways, then I will hear
from heaven, and will forgive their sin and heal their land.

2 Chronicles 7:12-14

PREPARATION

You will need five blocks from a child's set of blocks. Find
those which have the letters P, R, I, D, and E. On the reverse
side tape the letters L, O, V, and E.

Today is the day for us to talk about our country.
That's a good thing to talk about, isn't it? After all, we do
like it very much. We are happy to live in this land with
all the blessings God has given us.

Sometimes we forget that God gave us all those blessings. We like to think we deserve them. We even like to
think we know why. Perhaps it's because we have so
much energy. (*As you say this show the "E" block, then
place it so you will be able to put the other blocks on
top of it.*) We like to think we have more energy than
other people, so naturally we're a better country.

Or maybe we like to think, at least, that we're more
devoted to God. D is for devotion. We like to think that
we love God more than other people do and so he's
making us a better country. (*Again show this block and
place it.*)

Or sometimes we like to think it's because we work
harder, that we're more industrious. (*Show the "I"
block.*) If we work harder than other people do we naturally deserve something more. Or maybe our country
is a better country because we are very rich. (*Show the*

"*R*" *block*.) We do have many things, so we like to think we're better. Or maybe it's that we are more powerful than others. We're stronger people and a stronger country as well. (*Show the* "*P*" *block*.) We like to think we're really a great country.

But did you notice? When I put these things together, they spell a word, but it's not a very good word. (*By this time probably some of the children will have already known it and said it in response.*) That's right. It's pride, and pride is the sin that says "We are better than others." It's the sin that says "We deserve more than others." It's the sin that says, "We treat God better than do others."

But that means we're taking the credit and we're forgetting God. Pride always does that. That's why God would have us look in a different direction. He wants us to turn around from our sin of pride so that we can see something else. (*Turn the blocks around, so the word LOVE shows.*) What word do we see now? (*Wait for the response.*) That's right. It's love, and by that we mean God's love, and that's something different than our pride.

The good news about all this is that God in his love has sent his Son, Jesus Christ to us to turn us around. (*Cover the stack of blocks with your cross.*) On the cross God showed his great love for the whole world. His Son came to suffer and die to take away our sins of pride, and to open our eyes to God's love.

That makes everything different. If our country happens to have many blessings, it's not because we deserve them, but because God gives them. Our ideas should not be ideas of pride. Instead of pride, we can live in thanksgiving, and then we can even thank God for our country.

No More Tears

SCRIPTURE

Then I saw a new heaven and a new earth; for the first heaven and the first earth had passed away, and the sea was no more. And I saw the holy city, new Jerusalem, coming down out of heaven from God, prepared as a bride adorned for her husband; and I heard a great voice from the throne saying, "Behold, the dwelling of God is with men. He will dwell with them, and they shall be his people, and God himself will be with them; he will wipe away every tear from their eyes, and death shall be no more, neither shall there be mourning nor crying nor pain any more, for the former things have passed away."

Revelation 21:1-5

PREPARATION

The visual aids for this message are two mailing tubes. *(If large diameter mailing tubes of 3" diameter, so much the better. Otherwise, use the cardboard tubes from a household waxed paper roll or something similar).* Wrap each mailing tube with white paper and on them draw identical pictures or print sentences to indicate problems we sometimes know. These might be a child crying or a child in bed or a stick figure of a person with a broken arm. Use three or four illustrations. *(Use identical illustrations on each tube.)* Cut two pieces of white paper to fit on one end of each tube. On one, write the words JESUS IS WITH US and on the other write the word HEAVEN. *RAISED fro Th DEad* *(Use very bright colors for these, preferably reds and oranges.)*

We've often talked about the happy times we have in life. We know that there are many happy days, and many things we enjoy. We can't even count them all.

Sometimes, though, we aren't quite so happy. We have problems, too.

(Display the first mailing tube.) That's what I've tried to say on the outside of this little tube. Let's see what it tells us about our problems. *(Allow the children to identify the situations drawn and indicate their feelings about them.)* All of us feel that way sometimes, don't we? We do have problems.

But then it's a good thing to remember that we have

God's good news for those problem times. *(Have one of the children look through the tubes to the light to see the words JESUS IS WITH US.)* What was it you saw there? *(Wait for the response.)* Right. You saw the words "Jesus is with us." And even in our bad times it's good to know that Jesus is with us helping us with our problems.

But you know, that's only half of the good news. Let's look at this tube. It's just the same on the outside because it talks about those very same problems. But it is different. Who would like to look in this one? *(Allow one of the children to look.)* What did you see? That's right, you saw the word heaven. And why did you see the word heaven, do you suppose? *(Again wait for the response of the children.)* You are right. That is Jesus' promise. He will take us to ~~heaven.~~ RAISED from The Dead

That's the good news in both its parts. Jesus is with us now when we have our sad days and Jesus will take us to be with him at the resurrection when there will be no more sad days at all. Just think of that. That's his promise, and even when we have problems, we can stand them, with a promise like that.

Helping Each Other Love

SCRIPTURE

And let us consider how to stir up one another to love and good works, not neglecting to meet together, as is the habit of some, but encouraging one another, and all the more as you see the Day drawing near.

Hebrews 10:24-25 (Mother's Day)

PREPARATION

From red construction paper cut a 6" heart. On the one side print the words I LOVE YOU, and on the other side AND I LOVE YOU. From white paper, cut 3 folded 6" hearts, joined at the top so they can fold over the entire red heart described earlier. On the first of these white hearts put the words I DON'T WANT TO on each outer side. On the second one print the words I'M ANGRY and on the third, I DON'T LIKE YOU. Make one more double heart slightly larger than the others from a different color construction paper, preferably yellow, so that this heart can fold over and cover all the others. On this heart draw a simple cross on both sides.

Today's another one of those exciting days, isn't it? What day is it? *(Allow the children to answer. Probably all of them will remember that it is Mother's Day.)* And I suppose this morning most of us probably celebrated Mother's Day, didn't we? Maybe some of us did special things for her or some of us had special presents for her or some of us had special cards for her. *(You may wish to allow the children some time for interaction and response at this time.)*

All of those things are fun on Mother's Day aren't they? They're fun because they're a way of saying to our mothers, "Mother, I love you." In fact that's probably what our Mother's Day cards probably said, just as this heart does. *(Show it.)* When mother read our cards this morning, she probably said this. *(Turn the heart around, and wait for children to read.)*

That's a wonderful thing for God's people to say and

it's a beautiful way for God's people to live. The sad part is that that's not always the way we are.

When mother says to us "Please clean your room," and we'd rather watch TV, we sort of say "I don't want to." *(Cover the red heart with white heart number one.)* We cover up our love with it and we even make it hard for mother to love us.

Sometimes we become very upset *(repeat the action with white heart number two)* and we cover up our love with our anger.

Sometimes we even get so angry that we even say this *(show the words I DON'T LIKE YOU)* and again we cover up our heart with words like that. We cover up our love and we make it hard for others to love us. That's bad news!

But we have some good news to share. Even with our bad feelings God still has his love for us. *(Show the larger yellow heart and cover up the others with that.)* That's right. God's love covers all those feelings, all of our sins. God showed his love to us in one very special way. *(Point to the cross, inviting the children to react.)*

That's it. No matter how we feel about each other and how hard we make it for people to love us, God continues to do so. Jesus came to show that love to us.

That's our good news for Mother's Day. It gives us a new way to love mother and a new way for mother to love us. We can love each other with the love of Jesus. Really, though, that's good news for every day, because that's when we have Jesus' love.

Everything Under Control

SCRIPTURE

As he was now drawing near, at the descent of the Mount of Olives, the whole multitude of the disciples began to rejoice and praise God with a loud voice for all the mighty works that they had seen, saying, "Blessed be the King who comes in the name of the Lord! Peace in heaven and glory in the highest!"

Luke 19:37-38

PREPARATION

The visual aid for this short sermon is a marionette. If none is available you may substitute a jointed doll, tying strings to the hands and feet and connecting the strings to a control rod which you will hold. If no such jointed doll is available it is a simple matter to construct one from light cardboard, joining the limbs to the torso and the head to the body also with brass fasteners allowing all parts to move freely. Then connect the limbs and the head to a short control rod with strings.

I wonder how many of you know what I have this morning. What is this called? *(Wait for response.)* Very good, some of you do know. It's called a marionette, and it's fun to play with. The thing about a marionette that is so much fun is that I can make it do exactly as I please. *(Demonstrate as you explain.)* If I want this arm to move I pull this string; if I want this foot to move I pull this string. I can control everything the marionette does.

Now that's all right when we're playing with marionettes, but it isn't a good thing when we try to control each other. You see, we do like to control others. If we say to them, "Come here," we want them to come. If we say, "Do this," we want them to do it. If we say "Help me," we want them to help immediately. *(As you say these words, add emphasis to your sentences by pulling the strings, making the marionette function as you choose.)* We like to have everything and everyone under control.

That's the way the people were when Jesus came to Jerusalem on Palm Sunday. They were very happy and excited when he came into the city. They thought he would be a king they could control, who would give them just what they wanted. So they were disappointed when Jesus didn't produce exactly the things they hoped for. They couldn't control him. They felt just as we do when we can't control each other.

But the good news is that Jesus came to give us something more than the power to control each other. He gives us the power to love each other. In one way Jesus did allow himself to be controlled—when he died for our sins. He even went into the grave because of them, but that's the way he set us free. Our sins don't have to control us, and we don't have to control each other. We are not marionettes *(demonstrate it again);* we are people. We are his people.

The New Clothes

SCRIPTURE

And he said, "There was a man who had two sons; and the younger of them said to his father, 'Father, give me the share of property that falls to me.' And he divided his living between them. Not many days later, the younger son gathered all he had and took his journey into a far country, and there he squandered his property in loose living. And when he had spent everything, a great famine arose in that country, and he began to be in want. So he went and joined himself to one of the citizens of that country, who sent him into his fields to feed swine. And he would gladly have fed on the pods that the swine ate; and no one gave him anything. But when he came to himself and said, 'How many of my father's hired servants have bread enough and to spare, but I perish here with hunger! I will arise and go to my father, and I will say to him, "Father, I have sinned against heaven and before you; I am no longer worthy to be called your son; treat me as one of your hired servants."' And he arose and came to his father. But while he was yet at a distance, his father saw him and had compassion, and ran and embraced him and kissed him. And the son said to him, 'Father, I have sinned against heaven and before you; I am no longer worthy to be called your son.' But the father said to his servants, 'Bring quickly the best robe, and put it on him; and put a ring on his hand, and shoes on his feet; and bring the fatted calf and kill it, and let us eat and make merry; for this my son was dead, and is alive again; he was lost and is found.' And they began to make merry."

Luke 15:11-24

PREPARATION

The visual aid for this lesson is a paper doll with two sets of clothes. *If these are identical, the effect is even stronger.)*

This morning we're going to hear a story about a little girl named Susie. I don't know how old Susie was, but she was old enough to be very excited when the circus came to town, and her mother told her she could see the parade.

On the morning of the parade, Susie woke up very early, just like all of us do when something exciting happens. Right after breakfast, she asked her mother,

"Mother, is it time to go to the circus parade now?" Her mother said, "No, not yet, Susie." In a little while Susie asked again, "Is it time now?" and once more mother said, "No, not yet."

A few more minutes passed and then Susie asked, "May I get ready now, Mother?" Finally mother said, "Yes, you may get ready, but be very careful. Don't get dirty." So Susie got all ready to go to the parade. She even put on her nice clean clothes that mother had ready for her. *(Show the paper doll with its bright shiny clothes.)*

Soon Susie decided she would sit on the porch to watch. Then she decided she would walk to the end of her sidewalk to see if the parade might be coming. Before long she decided to go to the corner, and then to another corner, and then around another corner. But still, the parade didn't come.

Something else did, though. A car came by and hit a puddle of water in the street. Poor Susie! It splattered her new dress and made it all dirty. *(Mark her dress with a crayon.)*

Susie jumped back from the sidewalk and was going to go home when something else happened. She tripped and fell. Now her dress was not only dirty, but it was wrinkled, too. *(Wrinkle the dress on the paper doll as you say these words.)*

Saddest of all, though, as Susie discovered she didn't know where she was. She had gone too far.

What a sad story! Her dress was dirty and wrinkled and she was lost.

But then something very wonderful happened. Susie heard someone saying, "Susie, what are you doing way over here?" She looked up and saw her Uncle Bill. "Uncle Bill," she said, "I'm lost." Uncle Bill said "I think you must be. Come I'll take you home right now, but you're such a mess. *(Show the doll.)* Aren't you going to the parade?"

Susie looked at the dirt on her dress and at the wrinkles in her clothes and inside she began to cry. She felt sad all the way home.

But when Uncle Bill and Susie came up the sidewalk to her house, Susie's mother came out to meet them. "Oh Susie," she said, "where have you been? I've been so worried about you! And look at your clothes. They're such a mess. But I'm so happy you're home. Hurry, let's wash your face and hands and put on clean clothes again. Otherwise you'll miss the parade."

That's a happy ending for the story, isn't it? *(As you are saying this, take Susie's wrinkled dress off and put the new dress on her.)* But it's even more than a happy ending for Susie's story. It's for all of us. You see, God gave us a whole world to live in and told us to be careful with the way we live. But we aren't. We sin, and that's like getting our clothes dirty. We don't always listen to him. That's like running away from home. We're so far away though, we could never get back.

But that's our happy ending. Jesus came to bring us back. He came into our world to get us, to find us with all the dirt and the wrinkled clothes of our sins. With his cross he gives us something new. He gives us his love and he gives us his forgiveness. That's the new clothes we have, the new clothes in which we can be with him. It's even a happier ending for us. Susie got to see a circus parade, but we get to live with Jesus. He gives us the best robe we could have.

A Test for the Church

SCRIPTURE

Beloved, do not believe every spirit, but test the spirits to see whether they are of God; for many false prophets have gone out into the world. By this you know the Spirit of God: every spirit which confesses that Jesus Christ has come in the flesh is of God, and every spirit which does not confess Jesus is not of God. This is the spirit of antichrist, of which you heard that it was coming, and now it is in the world already. Little children, you are of God, and have overcome them; for he who is in you is greater than he who is in the world. They are of the world therefore what they say is of the world, and the world listens to them. We are of God. Whoever knows God listens to us, and he who is not of God does not listen to us. By this we know the spirit of truth and the spirit of error.

1 John 4:1-6

PREPARATION

From light cardboard stock cut five cards approximately seven inches by ten inches each. Draw a light line dividing four of the cards into two sections, and using felt markers or crayons prepare the following illustrations:

Card number one: On one side draw a large church building; on the other half, an identical building, much smaller. On the first half of card two, draw a large group of stick figures; on the other half a small group of similar figures. On card number three draw a very large dollar sign on the first half; a small dollar sign on the other. Draw a large staff and music notes on the first half of card number four; on the other side, a small staff and music notes. Draw a large cross in the center of card number five, with smaller drawings of the church building, the music staff, the people, and the dollar signs surrounding it.

This morning we are going to have a test for the church. That sounds funny, doesn't it? A test is something we have in school. But today, we're going to have a test for the church. Here are our test cards. On each one there is some thing about the church. We'll look at the cards, and test what sort of church we like.

(Show card number one.) Here is a picture of a church building. Really there are two pictures. Which one do

you think you'd rather belong to? *(Allow the children to answer. You may wish to lead them to the idea that bigger seems like better.)*

(Show the second picture.) Here are the people of the church. Again we can see that one church has many, many people and one church has only a few. *(Let your voice indicate disappointment.)* It would seem that this *(point to the larger group)* would be the better church, wouldn't it?

Or let's look at something else. *(Show card number three.)* We know that churches need money, and we thank God that his people give it. What do you think this card means? *(Allow the children to answer, again leading to the comment that a bigger amount of money seems to mean a better church.)*

Here is something else. *(Indicate the music staff.)* This means a church with a big choir and a big organ and many, many singers. *(Point to the large staff.)* And this one has just a small choir and a few singers. *(Point to the smaller staff.)* It would seem that this is the better church, wouldn't it?

It would seem that way because we often think that bigger and better are the same. They aren't. Not one of these cards really tells us about the church. We can't test a church by the size of its building, or the number of people. We can't find out whether it's a good church by the amount of money it has or the size of the choirs or how people sing. That's not the way to test the church.

But God told us in his word there is a way. We can tell whether the right things are happening in the church, but it's not through money or people or buildings or music. Instead it's this way. *(Show the final card with the cross in the center of the other things.)*

That's the test for the church. If Jesus is there with his cross, then it really is the church. The most important part of the church is the cross of Jesus.

We sometimes think bigger is better as we said, but that's just a sin of our pride. Jesus came to tell us that it's not being big that is best, but being forgiven. That he does with this. *(Point to cross.)*

This is the only test for the church: Is Jesus Christ shared with his love and his forgiveness? Where that love and forgiveness bring people to him and to each other, the church passes the test.

More Presents

SCRIPTURE

For to you is born this day in the city of David a Savior, who is Christ the Lord.

And when they saw it they made known the saying which had been told them concerning this child.

And the shepherds returned, glorifying and praising God for all they had heard and seen, as it had been told them.

Luke 2:11, 17, 20 (Christmas)

PREPARATION

Prepare three little Christmas gift boxes. Mark them as follows:

Something we need.

Something we share.

Something we do.

Inside box one place a cross. Inside the second box place a heart, and inside the third place a picture of the folded hands or a little piece of sheet music from a Christmas carol or any other symbol you might use to represent prayer and praise.

Christmas is exciting isn't it? We've had special songs and special clothes and special presents, too. I suppose all of us are excited about those presents. It's exciting to get presents, we know.

Today we're going to look at three presents God has for us. *(Show the boxes.)* Of course we know his big present to us is Jesus. We know Christmas is his birthday and these are his birthday presents to us.

(Show the first box and have someone read the inscription "Something we need.") Very good. This present is something we need. I wonder what that could be. Would you open it please? *(Ask a child to open it and show the cross.)* That is something we need. The angels told the shepherds "For unto you is born a Savior," and God tells us a Savior is something we need. We need his forgiveness.

26

Now let's look at the second package. Jesus is something we need. I wonder what something to share will be. Would someone like to open this? *(Have one of the children open it and display the heart.)* What does that mean? *(Wait for a response, perhaps leading to the idea of love.)* That is something to share isn't it? We can share the love Jesus gives us, just like the shepherds who shared their good news with everybody. We do have something to share, Jesus' love.

And now for our third present. This one says *(show label)* "Something to do." Who wants to open this one? *(Again choose someone to open the box and display what is inside.)* And what is our something to do? To pray, or to sing. To praise God, for his gift of Jesus.

That's our good news today. God has given us three presents: The Savior we need, his love to share, and his praises to sing. Merry Christmas.

He Sets Us Free

SCRIPTURE

And he came to Nazareth, where he had been brought up; and he went to the synagogue, as his custom was, on the sabbath day. And he stood up to read; and there was given to him the book of the prophet Isaiah. He opened the book and found the place where it was written, "The Spirit of the Lord is upon me, because he has anointed me to preach good news to the poor. He has sent me to proclaim release to the captives and recovering of sight to the blind, to set at liberty those who are oppressed, to proclaim the acceptable year of the Lord." And he closed the book, and gave it back to the attendant, and sat down; and the eyes of all in the synagogue were fixed on him. And he began to say to them, "Today this scripture has been fulfilled in your hearing."

Luke 4:16-21

PREPARATION

Cut a rectangular hole in the side of a shoe box as if it were to be a window, then place four cardboard strips vertically in that window to represent bars. (The box is to represent a prison cell with bars in the window.) On the strips print the words: "Afraid of God," "Afraid I'm a sinner," "Afraid I'm not important" and "Afraid of hell."

I wonder who can tell me what this box looks like this morning. Of course, we know it's a shoe box, but it's really meant to be something else and I wonder who can tell me what it is. (Wait for response.) That's right. It's a jail-room with bars on the window. They make it impossible for a person to get out.

But this is a different kind of prison. It's one that we live in; and these bars are our own. So let's see what they say. (Have the children read and wait for a response. You may wish to elaborate on each one very briefly.)

Those really are prison bars. Sometimes we're afraid of God, or afraid of our sins, afraid we're not very important people, or afraid of hell. Being afraid keeps us from being free and happy people. It's like being in prison.

But we have good news this morning, the good news that we don't have to live behind those bars at all. Jesus came to set us free. He came to show us that God loves us, and we don't have to be afraid. *(Remove the bar saying "Afraid of God.")* Jesus suffered and died to take away our sins. We don't even have to be afraid because we're sinners. We're forgiven. *(Repeat the process.)* God loves us so much that he sent Jesus to us. That makes us very important people. *(Remove that bar.)* Jesus did all of that for us, and we don't even have to be afraid of hell any more. *(Remove that bar.)*

That's the good news we have. Jesus has set us free, to be his people, to be alive and happy in his world. The bars are gone. Jesus removed them all with his cross.

The Easy Way

SCRIPTURE

Come to me, all who labor and are heavy-laden, and I will give you rest. Take my yoke upon you, and learn from me; for I am gentle and lowly in heart, and you will find rest for your souls. For my yoke is easy, and my burden is light."

Matthew 11:28-30

PREPARATION

You will need two boxes of approximately equal size. In the first, place three bricks. Label the first one RELIGIOUS RULES, the second WORK AT THE CHURCH, and the third MEETINGS TO ATTEND. In the other box place a large red heart and a cross. Label the box with the bricks MY RELIGION; label the box with the heart and the cross MY FAITH. *(As you begin this message have the boxes placed so that the labels cannot be seen.)*

I have two very important boxes to look at this morning. Here is one. *(Turn the first box around and wait for the response.)* Here is the other. *(Turn the other box and wait for that response.)*

They really seem almost the same, don't they? One says MY RELIGION and the other says MY FAITH. They are almost alike. At least we usually think they are. Let's see if there is a difference.

I would like someone to help me. *(Choose one of the smaller children who will obviously notice the weight difference of the boxes.)* Fine, I will pick Bonnie. Bonnie, will you please lift this box? *(Indicate the RELIGION box.)* Now lift this box. *(Indicating the FAITH box.)* What's the difference? *(Wait for Bonnie's response.)*

You are right; that box is a lot heavier. Let's find out why. *(Open the box.)* No wonder it's heavy. There are three bricks in it, and each brick has a label. *(Show them.)* This one is about RULES FOR RELIGION and this about WORK TO DO and this is about MEETINGS

30

TO ATTEND. Sometimes that's what religion seems to be, even though that might be a hard box to carry.

But let's look in the other box. *(Again choose a child, and wait for the response.)* This box is filled with God's love and his forgiveness. That's what faith is all about. *(Indicate label on box.)*

What a difference! Religion *(point to box)* can be the heavy rules we make ourselves. Faith is filled with our joy in God's love and his forgiveness. It means that Jesus took the whole heavy load of our sins. He makes life light and happy because he did.

Now, which box would you rather carry with you, the heavy load of religious things or the light load of his love?

Of course we do need some of these other things too. God does tell us how he would like us to live. And we do need to work for his kingdom, and there are some church meetings to attend. But as long as we remember these *(pointing to the cross and the heart)* then these aren't so heavy after all. Jesus makes them part of the fun of being his people. *(Tear the labels from the bricks and put them in the box marked FAITH.)* It's not heavy, after all.

The Light We Live

SCRIPTURE

This is the message we have heard from him and proclaim to you, that God is light and in him is no darkness at all. If we say we have fellowship with him while we walk in darkness, we lie and do not live according to the truth; but if we walk in the light, as he is in the light, we have fellowship with one another, and the blood of Jesus his Son cleanses us from all sin.

1 John 1:5-7

PREPARATION

The visual aid for this message is a small flip-chart. Page one will simply have the word LOVE, with beams of light appearing to radiate from it. Page two will be a divided page of black construction paper cut into four pieces so that each piece can be flipped down separately. Page three will be a cross, and page four the word LOVE once more with the cross superimposed on it.

This morning I have a little flip-chart to help us understand something about Christian life. You see, in the Bible God told us that living as his people is like walking in the light and showing his love is the same as showing his light. That's what we have on page one of our little chart. What is the word? *(Wait for response.)* And why do you think these little lines *(indicate the light rays)* are on the chart? Right. They tell us that walking in the light means showing God's love.

That's what we do, isn't it? We are his people. Jesus has made us his children and so we show his love.

Of course, that love doesn't always show. Sometimes it is hidden. We become angry. *(Flip down the first part of the black paper.)* Notice, some of our love is covered up. We disobey our parents and another part of the love is covered up. *(Repeat the action with a second part of the black paper.)* We tell a lie about someone *(repeat with the third part of the black paper)* or we pout when mother wants us to do something. *(Repeat with the final part of the black paper.)* But now do you see what has happened? Our sins have covered up all of the word LOVE. We can't see the love any more and we can't see the light. It's all dark.

That's the way sin is. That's the way our lives would be if God had just left us, covered up with darkness. But Jesus came to take that darkness away, to cover our sins with his love and his cross. *(Flip page three into place.)*

That's the good news God's people have. He took away the sins of our anger and our disobedience and our lying and our pouting and all our sins. Jesus made those his own and he gives us his love instead. *(Flip the fourth page into place.)* That means we are walking in the light again because Jesus has made us that kind of people. He gives us a new way to live and a new way to love. *(Show page one again.)*

The Bread that Spoils

SCRIPTURE

When they found him on the other side of the sea, they said to him, "Rabbi, when did you come here?" Jesus answered them, "Truly, truly, I say to you, you seek me, not because you saw signs, but because you ate your fill of the loaves. Do not labor for the food which perishes, but for the food which endures to eternal life, which the Son of man will give to you, for on him has God the Father set his seal."

John 6:25-27

PREPARATION

From light cardboard stock cut out five silhouettes of loaves of bread. On one paste a picture of a new bicycle. On another, paste new clothes; on another some money, and on another a drawing of a report card with all As. On the last one place the words JESUS CHRIST.

(Show the loaves of bread, with the pictures hidden.) Can anyone tell me what these are supposed to be? They represent something very important to us all. *(Wait for response, although you may have to prompt the children.)* That's right, these are loaves of bread, and bread is very important. We even call it the "staff of life." We need it.

Of course, we need other things, too. Today, these loaves of bread *(demonstrate them)* show some of them. Here is one. *(Show the bicycle.)* That's important, isn't it? We all like a good bicycle. Or this *(Show the next. Proceed with each loaf of bread, commenting or eliciting comments from the children on the things that you show.)*

We said before these are very important to us. The sad thing is that sometimes they become so important that we forget that these loaves of bread will spoil. A bicycle is very good to have, but it will wear out. New clothes are very fine, but they wear out, too. Having money is pleasant, but when we use it, it's gone. Even having a good report card seems important, and it is, but we forget reports cards, after a while. *(Crumple each loaf of bread as you speak about the particular item.)* That's what Jesus calls going after the bread that spoils. If these are the important things in life then we'll be disappointed. They will wear out and disappear.

That's why Jesus said, "I can give you something better. I can give you something that won't rust like a bicycle, or wear out like clothes, or disappear like money, or be forgotten like your grades. I can give you my love. That's the bread which never spoils. I can give you my forgiveness. That's the loaf which never disappears."

That is why Jesus came to the world. He came to turn us from making unimportant things, too important, to give us the bread that won't spoil. *(Show last card, with the cross.)*

With the Light Turned On

SCRIPTURE

"You are the light of the world. A city set on a hill cannot be hid. Nor do men light a lamp and put it under a bushel, but on a stand, and it gives light to all in the house. Let your light so shine before men, that they may see your good works and give glory to your Father who is in heaven.

Matthew 5:14-16

PREPARATION

Remove the lens cap from a flashlight. Cut a small piece of red construction paper to fit behind the lens and cut a heart from the center of this paper so that light shines through the heart. Replace lens cap.

Remove the batteries from the flashlight. Wrap one with a label saying THE WORD OF GOD. Wrap the other with a label saying THE SACRAMENTS. Begin your message with the batteries removed.

I have something very simple here which I think all of you recognize. (*Demonstrate the flashlight.*) It's a flashlight, a plain, simple, ordinary flashlight except for two things. One you can see on this end (*show the lens*) and one you can't see yet, but I'll tell you about it in a little while.

This flashlight is to remind us that Jesus said that we are to be the light of the world. That means we're to let his love shine through every one of us, just like it would in this flashlight. (*Show lens end again.*) Maybe one of you would like to demonstrate it. (*Give the flashlight to one of the children asking him to turn it on so the light can shine.*)

Oh, what's the matter? It's not working! The light isn't shining and I can't see the heart, can you? (*Do not continue this too long. The point is obvious, and some of the children will probably say very soon that there are no batteries.*)

(*Open the flashlight to verify.*) That's right. That's the

36

problem. The flashlight doesn't have batteries. That's just like us, too, It won't work by itself, and we can't be the light of the world by ourselves. We need power.

(Insert the batteries without indicating their labels, and invite one of the children to try it. Comment about the light, the heart, etc.)

Now let's see what kind of power makes our light shine. *(Open flashlight again and display the batteries with their labels.)* It's the power Jesus gives us in the word and the sacrament. *(You may wish to label the batteries simply JESUS' LOVE AND JESUS' FOR-GIVENESS. The point remains the same.)* That's the good news we have. Jesus is the light of the world, turning us on to show his love. Just think of that. Wherever we are his light can shine. He gives us that kind of power.

Do Not Disturb

SCRIPTURE

The Priests and the prophets and all the people heard
Jeremiah speaking these words in the house of the Lord. And
when Jeremiah had finished speaking all that the Lord had
commanded him to speak to all the people, then the priests
and the prophets and all the people laid hold of him saying,
"You shall die! Why have you prophesied in the name of the
Lord, saying, 'This house shall be like Shiloh, and this city
shall be desolate, without inhabitants?'" And all the people
gathered about Jeremiah in the house of the Lord.

When the princes of Judah heard these things, they came
up from the kings' house to the house of the Lord. Then the
priests and the prophets said to the princes and to all the
people, "This man deserves the sentence of death, because he
has prophesied against this city, as you have heard with your
own ears."

Then Jeremiah spoke to all the princes and all the people
saying, "The Lord sent me to prophesy against this house and
this city all the words you have heard. Now therefore amend
your ways and your doings, and obey the voice of the Lord
your God, and the Lord will repent of the evil which he has
pronounced against you."

Jeremiah 26:7-13

PREPARATION

Since this is an action message there will be no materials
to prepare. The only object necessary will be a cross.

This morning I'm going to ask all of you to help me.
I want you to close your ears when you hear something
you don't like to hear. First of all maybe you can show
me how you close your ears. (*Wait for the children to do
so and after they have done so, nod your head in ap-
proval.*) Very good.

Now, each time we hear something we don't like to
hear, we'll close our ears. Okay?

Let's pretend that we're playing, and for some reason
we push one of our friends down. When Mother comes
outside to find out what's wrong, she says, "Oh, but **you**

shouldn't do that. That was not good." *(Close your ears with those words.)*

Or, we're doing homework, and Sister tells us, "You've got it all wrong, and not only that, your paper's all messy too." We don't like to hear that, do we? *(Again, close your ears and wait for the children to do, also.)* That's right, we'd probably close our ears.

That's the way we are. We don't like to hear that we're wrong or that we have to change or that we've done something we shouldn't have done. We like to close our ears. That's easier than admitting we've been wrong.

That's the way God's people were in the Old Testament times when God sent one of his pastors to them to tell them they were wrong. They didn't want to hear. They didn't put their fingers in their ears as we just did, but they said they wouldn't listen.

We're still like that. We like to think we're perfect people. *(Puff up chest to act very impressive and pompous.)* We don't like it when the word of God tells us that we are sinners. We'd rather close our ears. *(Demonstrate the action.)*

That's why we need Jesus to come to us with his word. Of course he does open our ears first to tell us that we are sinners. But after he has opened our ears that way, then he opens them again so we can hear of his love. Jesus suffered and died to take away our sins, and that's something good to hear. *(Hold up the cross.)*

That's what Jesus does for us through his Word. He opens our ears to tell us about our sins, but then he opens them to tell us of his forgiveness. We don't have to keep our ears closed.

Our Pride and Our Prayers

SCRIPTURE

He also told this parable to some who trusted in themselves that they were righteous and despised others: "Two men went up into the temple to pray, one a Pharisee and the other a tax collector. The Pharisee stood and prayed thus with himself, 'God, I thank thee that I am not like other men, extortioners, unjust, adulterers, or even like this tax collector. I fast twice a week, I give tithes of all that I get.' But the tax collector, standing far off, would not even lift up his eyes to heaven, but beat his breast, saying 'God, be merciful to me a sinner!' I tell you, this man went down to his house justified rather than the other; for every one who exalts himself will be humbled, but he who humbles himself will be exalted."

Luke 18:9-14

PREPARATION

Prepare six folders to represent little prayer books. On the cover of each place a cross or a simple line drawing of folded hands. Inside folder one, print I THANK YOU LORD THAT I AM NOT AS SELFISH AS JACK. In folder two print, I THANK YOU LORD THAT I DO NOT LIE LIKE HENRY DOES. Folder three should have the words I THANK YOU THAT I GO TO CHURCH MORE THAN SUE; folder four, I THANK YOU THAT I HAVE A BETTER VOICE THAN JANE; and folder five, THANK YOU FOR MAKING ME A BETTER CHRISTIAN THAN MY FRIEND. Inside folder six print LORD JESUS, FORGIVE ME.

On the back of folder one, put the letter P; on the back of folder two the letter R; on folder three the letter I; on folder four, the letter D; on folder five the letter E. On the back of folder six place another cross.

It's so good to be in church again this morning! It's really fun to come together for Sunday school, and to sing and pray in church, isn't it? Sometimes we may get a little tired of it, but it really is good. It's especially good to know that we are God's people!

So, this morning we have some prayer books about being his people.

Here is the first one. Who would like to read this prayer for me? (*Choose a child to read the short prayer, continuing the process with each of the first five prayer books.)*

That's really something, isn't it? Each prayer book said "Thank you, Lord" for something. One of them says for being less selfish, or not lying as much, or going to church more, or having a better voice, or being a better Christian. But those are really imitation prayers, aren't they? Perhaps, if we turn the prayer books backwards we can see what they really are. *(Show the backs of the prayer books forming the word PRIDE.)*

That's right, they're not prayer words as much as they are pride words. Religious people sometimes have that kind of pride.

That's why we really need this other prayer book. *(Indicate the sixth prayer book.)* Let's read this one together. *(Permit children to respond. You may wish them to repeat it once or twice until they speak the words together.)* Now that's the real prayer, "Lord Jesus, forgive me."

It's very easy to be proud about being religious. Jesus even told a story about a man who was just like that, who prayed the same kind of prayers our first ones were. Then Jesus told us about another man who prayed this prayer that we prayed together, "Lord Jesus, forgive me."

He not only told about it. He had come into the world to suffer and die for our sins of pride too. He took all of our sins with him to the cross, and in his forgiveness we have a new way to pray.

God's Servant

SCRIPTURE

Let each of you look not only to his own interests, but also to the interests of others. Have this mind among yourselves, which you have in Christ Jesus, who, though he was in the form of God, did not count equality with God a thing to be grasped but emptied himself, taking the form of a servant, being born in the likeness of men.

Philippians 2:4-7

PREPARATION

You will need two strips of cardboard, the one approximately four inches by twelve inches, the other four inches by eighteen inches. On the longer strip print the words GOD'S SERVANT IN THE CHURCH, and on the other side place simple line drawings: the church, a Bible, music notes, perhaps a blackboard with chairs around it, a group of people together. On the shorter strip print the words GOD'S SERVANT IN THE WORLD. On the opposite side of that, line drawings of a dollar bill, several articles of clothing, several items of food, perhaps a window with bars around it to indicate a jail, or the door of a hospital.

This morning I would like someone to tell what a certain word means. The word is servant. What does it mean to be a servant? *(Wait for response. Allow children to discuss the word and dialogue with them.)*

That's right. A servant is someone who does something for someone else. A servant helps another person, works for him, does what he says. But did you know that we are servants?

We are God's servants, just as my little sign says. *(Show the longer strip which says GOD'S SERVANT IN THE CHURCH.)* These pictures tell us how we are servants for God. Let's see if we can name them. *(Have children name the line drawings you have indicated. You may wish to have them add more if their response indicates that sort of interest.)*

Very well done. These are things God's servants do,

if we are his servants in the church. But, this morning I'd like you to look at something else. *(Show the other card saying GOD'S SERVANT IN THE WORLD.)* God's servants do some things here in the church and do other things in their world, things like this. *(Show second card, and invite children to respond.)* Sometimes we think we are servants only in church.

But really we aren't God's servants all the way unless we serve both ways. We need both places. Let's see what happens if we put our signs together. *(Place the shorter strip about two thirds of the way up the longer strip. Allow the children to respond with the fact that we have made a cross.)* That's exactly it. If we are going to be a servant like Jesus was, then we're his servants in the church and in the world, too. That's the way Jesus came to serve us.

Where Is the King?

SCRIPTURE

Now when Jesus was born in Bethlehem of Judea in the days of Herod the king, behold, wise men from the East came to Jerusalem, saying, "Where is he who has been born king of the Jews? For we have seen his star in the East, and have come to worship him." When Herod the king heard this, he was troubled, and all Jerusalem with him.

Matthew 2:1-3

PREPARATION

From yellow construction paper prepare two crowns. The one should be very small, with a total diameter of four or five inches. The second should be quite large, with a diameter of twelve to fourteen inches. On each crown write the words JESUS IS KING. Prepare two collages, one to fit inside each crown. On the smaller collage include a Bible, a baptismal font, a view of a pulpit or a pew. (A church supply catalog may picture them.) On the larger collage include such items as toys, baseball, bats, gloves, bicycles, dolls, golf clubs, television sets, wallets, and almost anything which can represent life all around us.

When we celebrated Christmas, we noticed how shepherds came to worship the baby Jesus. Other people came too. The Bible tells us they were wise men, from the East. They didn't know where he was, so they asked: where is the king? That's a question for us, too.

Jesus is our king. (*Show the smaller crown.*) We do know where we can find him. We can find him right here, where these things happen. (*Show the smaller collage and invite the children to respond to the things they see.*)

That's right. Jesus is king right here. Here are all the places we find him and here are the ways that we see him.

And it's easy to have a king like that. It's especially easy to have Jesus as king if this is the only place we

44

find him. Then nothing else really matters. We can do what we want without ever seeing Jesus.

But, Jesus didn't come to be king just inside the church. *(Show larger collage.)* He came to be a king of everything we do, even when we play or watch TV or throw a football. He came to be a king of all things. *(Place the bigger crown over the larger collage.)*

That means we have a choice to make. We can have Jesus as the little king and keep him inside the church. *(Show small crown and collage.)* Or we can have Jesus as our real king, wherever we are and in whatever we do. *(Demonstrate with the larger crown and the collage once more.)*

Of course, that's really different. It means wherever we are, we are his people. That's a new way to live.

It was for that kind of crown Jesus came, because that's the kind of king he is. His throne was in a bed at Bethlehem, and on a cross near Jerusalem, and in life with his people everywhere.

And of course, that's good news! He is our king everywhere, touching us with his love and forgiveness in everything we do. We don't have to be satisfied with a small crown and a little king. *(Show the small crown.)* Our Jesus is king over everything.

We Need Each Other

SCRIPTURE

For the body does not consist of one member but of many. If the foot should say, "Because I am not a hand, I do not belong to the body," that would not make it any less a part of the body. And if the ear should say, "Because I am not an eye, I do not belong to the body," that would not make it any less a part of the body. If the whole body were an eye, where would be the hearing? If the whole body were an ear, where would be the sense of of smell? But as it is, God arranged the organs in the body, each one of them, as he chose. If all were a single organ, where would the body be? As it is, there are many parts, yet one body. The eye cannot say to the hand, "I have no need of you," nor again the head to the feet, "I have no need of you."

1 Corinthians 12:14-21

PREPARATION

Prepare two large paper doll figures, sixteen to eighteen inches high, preferably identical. Write children's names on the various parts of the bodies of each one. *(Use the same names for the same part on each doll. One arm might be John, the other, Henry; the head, Susan; the body, Anne; one foot, Tim, and so forth.)* Before this lesson is to be presented, place one paper doll out of sight, but where it will be easily accessible. *(You will begin this message with only one paper figure.)*

I think all of you can tell what I have in my hand. It's a paper doll. This morning, though, I'm going to ask you to pretend that this isn't a paper doll at all. Pretend it's a whole bunch of people, and each part is a different person.

So I've written different names on parts of this doll. Here is John and here is Susan. *(Continue pointing out the various parts you have named.)* You see all together all of these people make one body. That's even the way the Bible talks about the church. It says we're different people, making up one body.

Sometimes though, people aren't happy about their life with other people. One person says, "I don't want to be a part of that group" and he tears himself away. *(Tear off one of the arms.)* Or another says, "We don't need Tim in our group" and they put him aside. *(Tear off the part with his name. Continue until the entire body is dismembered.)*

But do you see what happened? Some people started feeling too important and others felt they weren't important enough, and our body has disappeared. All we have left are tiny little parts.

Sadly, that happens in the body of Christ, too. It happens when we think too much of ourselves or too little of each other. It happens when we aren't willing to accept each other or to work with one another. We tear the body apart. That's our sin.

We might ask how the church ever gets to be the body of Christ if we always tear it apart. That's a good question, and there's a good answer to it. It is the body of Christ, after all. He is the one who brings it together, even when we separate ourselves from each other. He suffered and died so that we wouldn't be such proud and separating people any more. His forgiveness takes away the sins which keep us torn apart. He puts his love in their place.

I can't put this body back together again, since I have torn it all apart. That's a miracle that only God can do. But I can show you with this new body the miracle he is doing for us. *(Show other doll.)* He does bring us together, to make us one. We're different parts, but together in him.

Pass It On

SCRIPTURE

But you shall receive power when the Holy Spirit has come upon you; and you shall be my witnesses in Jerusalem and in all Judea and Samaria and to the end of the earth.

Acts 1:8

PREPARATION

For this message you will need an envelope and a piece of church stationery. On the stationery print the words JESUS LOVES YOU and underneath that the words PASS THIS ON TO THE NEXT PERSON. Before you present this message though, secretly instruct one of the children to hold the letter in his hand after he has read it. As the children line up, be sure that this particular person is approximately in the center of the group.

This morning we need about eight or nine of you to help us share the word of God. Who would like to help? *(Choose them with the one you have instructed previously in the middle of the line.)*

Now I am going to give Anne this envelope. It has a message in it, and some instructions, too. Let's see what she does with it. Anne, here is the envelope. *(Watch as she opens it, reads it, folds it and passes it to the next person.)* Did you get the message, Anne? Very good. Let's see what Susan does.

(Continue with each of the children until it gets to the one who has been instructed to hold the letter.) Well, Heidi, the letter has stopped. What's the matter? What did the letter say? That's right! It said "God loves you." What else did it say? It said "Pass it on to the next person." Well, do you believe the first part? *(Allow Heidi to answer.)*

What about the second part? Why didn't you pass it on? *(She may respond, "Because you told me not to.")* That's right, I told you not to. I wanted to demonstrate what happens when we don't pass on God's love. None of these *(indicate the remaining children)* got to read it. That happened just because one person didn't pass the letter on.

God sent his love into the world in Jesus, and he tells us to pass that on. Sadly, like Heidi with the letter, we keep it to ourselves too much. Perhaps we're too tired, or perhaps too shy, or perhaps, even afraid.

So we need the love God sent us, too. Jesus tells us he came to pass that love to us, and he will do it through us. Being tired or shy or afraid is nothing when we have Jesus' power. That's something to pass on.

It's Good to Be Here

SCRIPTURE

Now about eight days after these sayings he took with him Peter and James, and went up on the mountain to pray. And as he was praying the appearance of his countenance was altered, and his raiment became dazzling white. And behold, two men talked with him, Moses and Elijah, who appeared in glory and spoke of his departure, which he was to accomplish at Jerusalem. Now Peter and those who were with him were heavy with sleep but kept awake, and they saw his glory and the two men who stood with him. And as the men were parting from him, Peter said to Jesus, "Master, it is well that we are here; let us make three booths, one for you and one for Moses and one for Elijah"—not knowing what he said. As he said this, a cloud came and overshadowed them; and they were afraid as they entered the cloud. And a voice came out of the cloud saying, "This is my Son, my Chosen; listen to him!" And when the voice had spoken, Jesus was found alone. And they kept silence and told no one in those days anything of what they had seen.

Luke 9:28-36

PREPARATION

From a cardboard box construct a replica of a church. (It need not be a particular church but one which can be identified, perhaps with its arched windows or the arched doorway or a steeple.) The back of the box should be open so that you can reach in for the cards you will need.

Prepare two cards to fit into the church. On one, mark a large cross on one side, and many small crosses on the other On the second card, make a large heart on one side, and many small hearts on the reverse side.

Who can tell me what this is? I know it's a box, but it's supposed to be something special. (*Wait for children to respond. You might point to the arched windows, etc., finally indicating that it is supposed to be a church.*)

Of course we know that a box isn't a church, not even the box we're in right now. The church is people, and our building is just where we come to be the church and to do what the church does. We come together to sing and to pray and to praise God. We come together to share his love *(show the large heart and then place it back inside the church)* and we come together to share his forgiveness. *(Repeat the action with the cross.)* That's why it's so good to be here. It's good to share Jesus' forgiveness and it's good to share God's love.

But it would be wrong if we just stayed here with that love, or if we thought that only here could Jesus' forgiveness be real for us. We do have his forgiveness here *(show the card with the large cross)* but we leave here to take it to everyone else who needs it. *(Show little crosses.)*

We do have God's love here and we know it, *(show the large heart)* but we can't stay here with that love either. *(Turn card around.)* We go from here to other people who need his love too, wherever they might be. With our hearts filled here, we go to share with others.

So we want to say, "It's good to be here," but especially we want to say, "We can't stay." Jesus sends us out with his forgiveness and his love. It's good to be here where he is. It's good to be there *(indicate area around church)* because he is there too. And when we are there with these *(show crosses and hearts)* we are there with him.

Which Crown?

SCRIPTURE

But seek first his kingdom and his righteousness, and all these things shall be yours as well.

Matthew 6:33

PREPARATION

Make two crowns from construction paper, each large enough to fit over a child's head. On the one, print: JESUS IS KING, I WILL LOVE HIM, I WILL LEARN ABOUT HIM, I WILL TELL OTHERS, I WILL GIVE TO HIM, I WILL LOVE OTHERS. On the other crown write these sentences: I AM KING, I LOVE MYSELF MOST, I KNOW ENOUGH, WHY SHOULD I TELL OTHERS, I WANT TO KEEP WHAT I HAVE.

This morning we're going to look at two different crowns. You know what a crown is, don't you? *(Wait for children to respond.)* A crown is something a king wears. But this morning we have two crowns, because we're going to be talking about two different kings. Here is one crown. *(Place the crown on a child's head, so the words JESUS IS KING face the front and the other children. Have the children read the other sentences on the crown.)* You see we're Jesus' children so our crown can say JESUS IS KING. And we can say all of these other things we read about loving him, learning about him, loving others, and so on. Jesus is really our king.

But sometimes we take this crown away *(do so)* and we put another in its place. *(Place the other crown on the child's head.)* Do you notice the difference? The first one said "Jesus is King," but this one says: "I am king." And that makes everything different. Let's look at the other sentences. Perhaps you can read them. *(Permit the children to read each of the sentences on this crown.)*

Do you see? They're exact opposites. The sad part is that sometimes we like to wear this crown. *(Point to the one which says I AM KING.)*

But that's why Jesus wore a different crown for us all. He wore a crown that had thorns in it, when he suffered and died for us. His throne was different too. It was a cross. But with all of his suffering and with that crown of thorns and that throne of the cross, Jesus took away our sins. He took away our sin of wanting to be king, and of wanting to live for ourselves, and to keep everything for ourselves. Those sins are gone. Jesus took them away. Since he did, he can wear this crown *(show crown number one)* and we can say Jesus is our King.

Whose Sins Are Bigger?

SCRIPTURE

Judge not, that you be not judged. For with the judgment you pronounce you will be judged, and the measure you give will be the measure you get. Why do you see the speck that is in your brother's eye, but do not notice the log that is in your own eye? Or how can you say to your brother, "Let me take the speck out of your eye," when there is a log in your own eye? You hypocrite, first take the log out of your own eye, and then you will see clearly to take the speck out of your brother's eye.

Matthew 7:1-5

PREPARATION

Prepare four flash cards as follows:

Number 1. On side one print SUSIE WAS NAUGHTY in very large letters. On the reverse in very small letters print I WAS NAUGHTY TOO.

Number 2. In large letters print TIMMY LEFT HIS ROOM A MESS; on the reverse side in small letters MY ROOM IS MESSY TOO.

Number 3. Print TOMMY DIDN'T MIND HIS MOTHER in large letters. On the reverse, print I DIDN'T MIND MY MOTHER, EITHER, in small letters.

On the fourth card print these words on the front: WE ARE ALL SINNERS; on the reverse side draw a cross.

This morning we're going to do something that is very easy and we're going to do something that is very hard. These cards will tell us both what is easy and what is hard.

(*Show the first card.*) Would somebody read this for me please? (*Permit child to read.*) Well, I said we would do something easy. That was really an easy thing to do. Did you notice how big these letters are? That's to show us how easy it is to tell when somebody else is naughty. But now we'll do something hard. (*Turn the card around.*) What does this side say? (*Have same child read.*) But do you see a difference? These are very small letters. Do you know why? They're small because it's harder for us to admit that we are naughty too. It's easy to see some other person being naughty, but it's harder to see in ourselves.

Or look at this card. *(Repeat the procedure, using the second card and the third, making similar comments to those you have made with the first.)*

That's a problem even God's people have. It's easy to see the sins of others and hard to see our own. Jesus even talked about that when he said that you can find a little speck of dust in your friend's eye, but you can't see a big piece of wood that's in your own.

But Jesus said that's not the way his people are to live. It's wrong when we make the sins of others big and it's wrong when we make our own sins so small. We have a different way to see things. This is the way God's people see. *(Show card four, inviting comment as you do.)* That's it. We are all sinners. Susie's sins and Timmy's sins and Tommy's sins and Henry's sins and Mary's sins and my sins are all alike.

And it shows us something else. We're really alike, and we need the same thing. We need the forgiveness Jesus brought to his world. *(Turn the card so the cross shows.)* Jesus gives it to us from his cross. That's good news.

There's more good news too. We don't have to make other people's sins bigger or pretend our sins are smaller. Jesus came to take them all away. He opens our eyes to our sin, *(show the card)* and opens our eyes to his cross.

Nice People — New People

SCRIPTURE

For I tell you, unless your righteousness exceeds that of the scribes and Pharisees, you will never enter the kingdom of heaven.

Matthew 5:20

PREPARATION

Cut a cardboard silhouette to represent a church building. Attach an envelope behind it to hold the flash cards you will use in the presentation.

The flash cards should have the following texts:

Card number one: Nice people don't kill.

Card number two: Nice people don't steal.

Card three: Nice people don't lie.

Card four: Picture of Christ.

Card five: New people need the Word.

Card six: New people need the Sacrament.

This morning we're going to look at the church. *(Show silhouette.)* This is supposed to be the church. Of course, we know that a building isn't the church. It's only a building where people come to be the church. So, if we're going to look at the church, we're really going to have to look at people.

And there's one thing we can say about the church's people. They are nice people, isn't that right? *(Nod your head, to encourage children to nod in response.)*

There are some things we can say about nice people, too. Here's one. *(Show card number one, drawing comments from the children as you do. Repeat with cards two and three.)* Those are really true, aren't they! And they are true for us, too. None of has killed anyone, or at least I hope not. None of us has stolen anything. We don't tell lies, at least not very big ones. We are really nice people, aren't we? *(As you say these words, again nod your head in affirmation. You may be surprised at the affirmative response.)* That's it, we're nice people, right?

Wrong.

(Pretend surprise.) What? Does that mean we're not nice people? Well, let's see. It's true, nice people don't kill but Jesus said to his disciples that killing isn't the only sin. He said that being very angry with someone is the same thing as killing. Or it's true that nice people don't steal, but Jesus said even wanting something someone else has is the same thing. And it's true nice people don't lie very much, but do you know that even a little fib is really something wrong?

The church is not filled with nice people after all. The church is filled with people who know they are not so nice. The church is for people who are sinners, who need something to make them different and new. And that's what Jesus does. *(Show picture.)*

That's why the church is for new people, not just nice people. New people are the ones Jesus has touched with his love. New people are those in whom Jesus is working his forgiveness. New people are those to whom Jesus is sending his Holy Spirit, making us the kind of people he wants us to be.

And now we can really see why we need the church. We don't need it because we're such nice people. *(Show card.)* We need it because we are new people, and new people need the Word of God to keep them new. *(Show card.)* New people need the sacrament to keep their newness alive.

So it's sort of a choice, isn't it? Which would you rather be? Just nice or really new? The good news is that Jesus is with us, and we are his new people.

With Eyes Wide Open

SCRIPTURE

With eyes wide open to the mercies of God, I beg you, my brothers, as an act of intelligent worship, to give him your bodies, as a living sacrifice, consecrated to him and acceptable by him. Don't let the world around you squeeze you into its own mold but let God remold your mind from within, so that you may prove in practice that the plan of God for you is good, meets all his demands and moves toward the goal of true maturity.

Romans 12:1-2
(Phillips)

PREPARATION

The two objects needed for this message are a heart and a cross.

This morning I am going to ask all of you to help me by closing your eyes for a very short time. Will you do that now, please? *(Wait for the children to close their eyes.)* That's right. Now, how much can you see? *(Wait for answers indicating that they see nothing.)*

Now, let's try something else. Let's open our eyes just half way. *(Again wait for the children to respond, and converse with them as they do so.)* That's right, now we can see a little, but we really can't see clearly, can we?

Let's try something different now. Let's open our eyes all the way and look around. Now, what can we see? *(Again, wait for the response.)* That's right. When we have our eyes wide open then we can see everything around us.

Now please close your eyes tightly once more. *(After all have their eyes closed hold the cross and the heart before them.)* What do you see? Of course, you see nothing, because your eyes are closed.

But now, let's open our eyes just half way. *(As they do so, hold up the cross and the heart once more.)* What do you see now? Very good. Some of you can see the heart and some of you can see the cross. When our eyes are half open we can see them, but we can't see them very well. But at least we know they are there.

Now let's open our eyes all the way. *(Wait, then show the heart and the cross.) What a difference!* Now we can see these very well. I wonder who remembers what the heart means? *(Wait for the response that it means God's love.)* Who can tell me what this cross means? *(Again wait for the response.)* That's it. When our eyes are wide open, we can see God's love and his forgiveness.

The sad part is that we don't always have our eyes wide open. Sometimes we get so busy with other things that we close our eyes to his love. *(Demonstrate facially.)* Sometimes we get so concerned about other things, our eyes go half closed and we don't see his forgiveness. Sometimes we keep our eyes so wide open to the TV or the ball games or to the other things we do that they're only half open to the things God does.

That's why this is such good news for us. *(Show cross.)* We can say that maybe that's the reason Jesus came to our world. He opens our eyes to the love God has for us. He does this with his forgiveness for our half-closed eyes. When we see the cross, we can see God's love. We'll have our eyes wide open.

It's What's Inside that Counts

SCRIPTURE

Blessed are the pure in heart, for they shall see God.

Matthew 5:8

PREPARATION

You will need two identical boxes, labeled in the same way. The front should say: I AM A CHRISTIAN. Around the box are to be other sentences describing Christian activity, such as I GO TO CHURCH, I GO TO SUNDAY SCHOOL, I PRAY, I SING, I READ THE BIBLE, I GIVE. *(These activities may vary to reflect your own particular emphasis. The boxes should be labeled identically.)*

One box is to be empty.

Inside the other box should be a heart with the words I AM A SINNER on one side and I HAVE JESUS' FORGIVENESS on the other.

I have two boxes to look at this morning. As you look at them I think you can tell me something about them. What do they say? *(Wait for response.)* Is there much difference? *(Again wait for the children to respond. You may wish to have children read the various sentences, indicating as they do how similar the boxes are.)*

Perhaps we could call these Christian boxes. They really talk about Christian things, don't they? These labels say I AM A CHRISTIAN, and both boxes have the same sentences about things Christians do. They are Christian boxes and very much alike.

Perhaps we shouldn't say that. Maybe they just seem to be alike on the outside. *(Shake the box to demonstrate that the one obviously has something inside it.)* Oh, now we find there's something different. What could that difference be? *(Again wait for the children to respond.)* All right, let's open it. *(Do so, opening the empty one first.)* No, there's nothing in there.

So let's open this one. *(Do so, allowing one of the children to lift the heart from the box.)* There was something in it after all, wasn't there? What is it? *(Wait for response.)* What does it say? *(Again, wait for response.)* The boxes really are different after all.

Maybe that should tell us something. On the outside people are like our two boxes. They seem to be the same. But what's inside really counts. We can act like Christians on the outside. But we need this *(show the first side of the heart)* and this *(show the other side.)*

Perhaps we should ask what makes the difference inside a Christian? Here is the answer. *(Point to the word JESUS.)* It's Jesus who makes the difference. Jesus comes to live inside us with his word. He calls us to confess our sins, and gives us his forgiveness.

The outside is the very same, isn't it? It's what's inside that counts. We can thank Jesus for the difference he makes inside us.

Growing-up Christians

SCRIPTURE

His divine power has granted to us all things that pertain to life and godliness through the knowledge of him who called us to his own glory and excellence, by which he has granted to us his precious and very great promises, that through these you may escape from the corruption that is in the world because of passion, and become partakers of the divine nature. For this very reason make every effort to supplement your faith with virtue, and virtue with knowledge, and knowledge with self-control, and self-control with steadfastness, and steadfastness with godliness.

2 Peter 1:3-8

PREPARATION

Tape the edges of a file folder together to form a double card. Cut five small doors through the front card of the folder so that each door can be opened to show a word printed behind it. Print the following words at the various doors: FAITH, KNOWLEDGE, SELF-CONTROL, CONCERN, and LOVE. On the inside of each doorway which will show when the door is open, make a cross.

All of us are God's people, aren't we? Of course we are. Jesus made us the people of God with his love to us and his forgiveness for us. That's really good news always.

And God's people have many opportunities to grow up as his people. On this card *(show the card)* are doors which show some of these opportunities. Behind every one of these little doors is something we can do while we grow up.

Who would like to open the first door? *(Indicate the first door marked FAITH, and invite one of the children to open it.)* That's right. That's a doorway to doing Christian things. If we're going to grow up as God's people, faith is the beginning. *(Point to the cross showing on the door.)* That's the first gift of Jesus to us. We can believe in him because he came to be our Savior.

Now let's try door number two. *(Repeat the process with each door, connecting the Christian virtue demonstrated and the cross, which is behind each door. The point for each one of the virtues is simply this: we have this as the gift of Jesus Christ. His cross opens the door for us, and each one means some growing up.)*

So now we look in our doorways. I wonder who can name all the things which mean we are growing up? *(Wait for the children to name them. They may need some prompting.)* But more important than naming them is living them!

And that's the good news we have. Jesus entered our world. His doorway was the manger at Bethlehem, and he opens doors for us with that cross from Jerusalem. We can live as growing-up Christians.

Something's Hidden

SCRIPTURE

Since we have such a hope, we are very bold, not like Moses, who put a veil over his face so that the Israelites might not see the end of the fading splendor. But their minds were hardened; for to this day, when they read the old covenant, that same veil remains unlifted, because only through Christ is it taken away. Yes, to this day whenever Moses is read a veil lies over their minds; but when a man turns to the Lord the veil is removed.

2 Corinthians 3:12-16

PREPARATION

Over a cross, either an actual cross or a drawing of one, tape five pieces of waxed paper. On one piece print the word TRADITION, and another RULES, on another PEOPLE MIGHT NOT LIKE IT, on another LAZINESS, and on another PRIDE. *(You may have to experiment with different marking pens; many will not print on waxed paper.)*

This morning again we're going to talk about what it means to be the people of God. But perhaps we could say that in a different way. We could talk about some of the troubles we have in being the church. It's almost the same. The church is the people of God.

Maybe we could ask what makes the church the church. Let's see what ideas we have. What is the main idea of the church? *(Invite the children to share their ideas. They will offer many; comment on each, gradually leading to the cross.)* That's right, we've named many important things, and the most important is the cross of Jesus. *(Show the cross, with the waxed paper held back.)*

It's sad though that sometimes we sort of cover up the cross with other things. *(Place the first piece of waxed paper in place.)* Here is one called TRADITION. Does anybody know what traditions are? *(Invite the children to give their answers.)* A tradition is something that we always do, repeating what we've done in the past. Tradition can become more important than the cross.

64

Or here is another one called RULES. They can get in the way of the cross too, when they become more important than sharing the good news about Jesus.

Here's another one, I wonder who would like to read it. *(Invite them to read PEOPLE MIGHT NOT LIKE IT.)* Well that's a strange one. Can that cover up the cross too? Yes, sometimes it can. We become more concerned about what people like than about what God says.

Here is something else. *(Indicate the word LAZINESS.)* When we are too lazy to do the work of Jesus the cross gets covered. So with this one too, when we are so proud of our church or our building or our comfortable pews or our organ. They become more important than the cross. It gets hidden behind them all.

These are the sins of all people, God's people too. We may not mean to cover Jesus' cross, but still we do.

But you'll notice something; Jesus doesn't allow his cross to be covered completely. It's still there. Wherever the church has the word of God and the sacraments, there is Jesus with his cross. And with his cross, and his suffering and death, Jesus takes away our sins, even those of covering him up. He took our pride as if it were one of his sins. *(Remove that piece of waxed paper.)* He came, not to be lazy but to work the will of God for us. *(Remove that paper.)* Jesus wasn't worried about what people liked. He brought them God's love. *(Remove the third waxed paper sheet.)* He reached past rules and regulations to offer people forgiveness. *(Remove that piece of paper.)* He even set aside the traditions so that his people might know his great love. *(Remove the last.)*

Now what do we have left? We have the cross. That's where we started in the first place. The good news about it now, is that Jesus forgives us, and the cross isn't hidden any more.

Being Important

SCRIPTURE

My brethren, show no partiality as you hold the faith of our Lord Jesus Christ, the Lord of glory. For if a man with gold rings and in fine clothing comes into your assembly, and a poor man in shabby clothing also comes in, and you pay attention to the one who wears the fine clothing and say, "Have a seat here, please," while you say to the poor man, "Stand there," or, "Sit at my feet," have you not made distinctions among yourselves, and become judges with evil thoughts?

James 2:1-4

PREPARATION

Prepare four sets of pictures, using the items suggested or others of your own preference.

On set one, picture a deluxe model ten-speed bicycle; on the other one of that set a very simple and plain bicycle. On set two, show a large, color TV home entertainment center; on the other card, a small black and white television. Set three should illustrate a very large, expensive automobile contrasting with a low cost model on the other card. Set four should picture a $100 bill; on the matching card, a dollar bill.

You will also need a plain cross.

We all like to be important people. We even find different ways to be important. Sometimes our importance comes through our good grades or sometimes through being very popular, or sometimes through having many things.

These pictures show us some things that we think make us important. For example, here are two pictures. *(Demonstrate set one.)* This is really a deluxe bike, isn't it? This one isn't. Which do you think makes a person more important? Usually we believe the better bicycle makes us more important.

Or let's look at this set of pictures. *(Repeat with sets two, three, and four, making appropriate comments as you do.)*

You see, that's the way we are. We think we're important because of the things we have. We even say:

"My bike's better than your bike," or something like that. But that's exactly the wrong way to be important. In fact, God told us in his word it's the wrong way to look at other people as well as at ourselves.

It's really a sign of our sin when we think things make us important. It's another sin when we think other people are important because of the things they have. People are important for themselves, not for things.

You see, bicycles will wear out; both kinds will. *(Demonstrate the picture.)* Or television sets will burn out. *(Demonstrate that picture.)* Cars get old, and even money disappears. None of these are the most important things of life because they can't last as long as we live.

But there's even a more important reason none of these things can make us important. A bicycle is great to have, but it can't love us. Cars are fine, but they can't have any feeling for us. Television sets can entertain us, but they can't be friends. *(Demonstrate the cards.)* These are all good things to have, but they're only things. There must be a different way to be important.

And that's the good news for the people of God. There is a different way to be important. It's this way. *(Demonstrate the cross.)* That's right. It's the cross of Jesus that makes us important. We were so important to Jesus that he died to bring us forgiveness.

And that's our good news today. Our baptism makes us children of God and that's important. We have God's love and we have God's forgiveness. They are important, and they will last forever. That's important, too. We don't have to try to be important through the things we have. We are important because of the love Jesus has for us.

Not Always Easy

SCRIPTURE

And he called to him the multitude with his disciples, and said to them, "If any man would come after me, let him deny himself and take up his cross and follow me. For whoever would save his life will lose it; and whoever loses his life for my sake and the gospel's will save it. For what does it profit a man, to gain the whole world and forfeit his life? For what can a man give in return for his life? For whoever is ashamed of me and of my words in this adulterous and sinful generation, of him will the Son of man also be ashamed, when he comes in the glory of his Father with the holy angels."

Mark 8:34-38

PREPARATION

From construction paper cut a crown, either to place on your own head or as a silhouette. You will also need a cross, possibly cut from the same color construction paper.

Sometimes when Jesus talked to his disciples, he said some very strange things and some very hard things. For example, he said if we want to follow him we should take up our cross to do so. (*Lift the cross in front of the children.*) That is a hard thing because taking up a cross for Jesus means doing things that will not be easy.

Our problem is that we like to do things the easy way. We don't like doing things that are difficult or that would make us unpopular. We would rather have an easy way. We'd rather have a crown than a cross. (*Demonstrate holding the crown in front of the children.*)

For example, when it's lunch time at school, it's hard to bow our heads and ask Jesus to bless our food or thank him for it. With all the other kids around we feel that they might laugh at us, so rather than pick up the cross, which would be praying even if they do laugh, we take the easy way. We'd rather have a crown than a cross. (*Demonstrate.*)

Or, to talk about loving all people is easy. But when a

boy of another color in our class needs some help, we have trouble. He's a different color, after all. So we take the easier way. We don't want to take the cross; we'd rather have a crown. *(Again demonstrate the actions.)*

There are other ways too. Instead of coming to church and Sunday school, we say Sunday is the only day we can sleep. We're pushing the cross away. *(Do so visually.)* When we're selfish with our things, we're pushing the cross away again. *(Again, demonstrate the action.)* When there's something to do to help our parents, and we play ball instead, it's a way of pushing the cross aside. *(Again demonstrate.)*

That's bad news. But that's the way we are. We don't like to do things that are difficult or not quite pleasant. We'd rather have the easy way. We'd rather have a crown than a cross.

But if that's our bad news, we have good news too. We have the good news that Jesus chose the cross instead of the crown. He took up his cross to show his love for us. He died to give his forgiveness to us. He even forgives us our sin of not wanting to take up the cross, of looking for the easy way.

When we have that love and that forgiveness in Jesus, we really have something different. We have the cross and the crown. We have the cross of his forgiveness and the crown of his love. That means we can take up crosses and follow him. We have Jesus and we don't have to look for the easy way.

Bridges or Fences?

SCRIPTURE

I do not pray for these only, but also for those who believe in me through their word that they may all be one even as thou, Father, art in me, and I in thee, that they also may be in us, so that the world may believe that thou hast sent me. The glory which thou hast given me I have given to them, that they may be one even as we are one.

John 17:20-22

PREPARATION

From either light wood or cardboard stock make a fence section using two end posts and four boards to serve as the fence section itself. On one side of the boards write the words LOVE, CONCERN, FORGIVENESS, JESUS CHRIST. On the opposite side of the same boards write the words SELF-CENTERED-NESS, SELFISHNESS, JEALOUSY, and FEAR.

(As the children come forward, hold the fence section vertically so the words SELF-CENTEREDNESS, SELF-ISHNESS, etc. appear to the children.) I wonder if anyone can tell me what I have this morning. *(Demonstrate the fence.)* Don't look at these words, but just tell me what you think this is supposed to be. *(Wait until the children respond.)* That's right. It's part of a fence. And the way I'm holding it right now, it separates us from each other. There's a fence between us. I have put it there.

On each one of the fence boards there are things that keep us apart. Would someone like to read the first one? *(Pick a child, then repeat with each one of the "boards" of the fence section.)* These are the things that make fences between people. They separate us from each other.

Sadly, that's the way many of us like to live. We think of ourselves first. *(Point to the first board.)* Or we want to keep everything for ourselves. *(Point to the second board. Continue with all the planks using illustrations as you choose.)* That's the way we build fences.

But that's not the way Jesus wants his people to live. He wants us to be with each other rather than separated from one another. He wanted us to build bridges rather than fences. *(Demonstrate by turning the fence section flat, the words of LOVE and CONCERN showing at the top, as if they are a bridge between you and the children.)* Now we have a bridge. With the love Jesus gives us, we can be loving to each other. With his concern, we can be concerned about each other. With his forgiveness we can forgive one another. Jesus lives in us, and we can live with each other.

That's the good news we celebrate today. That's a real reason for happiness. Jesus Christ made a bridge out of his cross to reach us and to break down our fences. We don't have fences keeping us apart. We have bridges bringing us together.

Fading Love

SCRIPTURE

To the angel of the church in Ephesus write: "The words of him who holds the seven stars in his right hand, who walks among the seven golden lampstands.

"I know your works, your toil and your patient endurance, and how you cannot bear evil men but have tested those and found them to be false; I know you are enduring patiently and bearing up for my name's sake, and you have not grown weary. But I have this against you, that you have abandoned the love you had at first. Remember then from what you did at first. If not I will come to you and remove your lampstand from its place, unless you repent."

Revelation 2:1-5

PREPARATION

Prepare a folder to represent a four page book. The title page should be "A Book About Love."

The pages will be as follows:

Page one, a bright red heart covering most of the page; page two, a smaller heart with the color much lighter than page one; page three, a still smaller heart with the color almost gone.

Also prepare a similar book with the same title page, but page one should have a large heart with the cross in the center. The heart on page two should be a little larger and page three, larger still. The cross and the color should be equally intense on all these hearts.

This morning we're going to look at two little books I have made. Who would like to tell me the name of these books? *(Choose one of the children to read the title of the book.)*

First we will look at this book. It's a book about love, but it's about our kind of love and what can happen to it. Let's see what it says.

This heart is a sign that we love God. Of course we do. That's why we're here this morning. This heart shows that love. Look how big and bright it is. That's a good kind of love.

But let's see what can happen. *(Show page two elicit-*

ing comments from the children. Then show page three and again draw more comments.)

That's right. The hearts faded away. They got smaller and smaller, and weren't nearly as bright. That's a sad kind of love, isn't it?

But it can happen. Our love can fade away. If we stay away from Jesus, or if we don't hear his word, or if we don't share his love, our love fades away. *(Show pages of the book.)*

But let's see what happens with Jesus' love for us. *(Show book two, demonstrating page after page, eliciting the comments of the children.)* Did you notice? These books are different. The hearts are different. These have a cross in the center. That means they show Jesus' love for us.

And that love doesn't get smaller, it doesn't fade away. Instead it got brighter and brighter and bigger and bigger, because that's the way Jesus shares his love with his people. The more we have of it, the more our love grows.

So that's our word for today. With the cross Jesus takes away our sins of fading love. *(Point to book one and then the cross.)* And with his love he makes our love bigger and brighter. *(Turn the pages of book two.)*

When We Are Sad

SCRIPTURE

Blessed are those who mourn, for they shall be comforted.

Matthew 5:4

PREPARATION

From heavy paper or light cardboard prepare two simple masks. These can be nothing more than egg-shaped faces with eye holes and a mouth. One mask should have a smiling mouth; the other, a sad one.

All of us like to be happy, don't we? We like our faces to look like this, *(demonstrate the happy face)* and most of the time they can. We have the things we need, we have friends to play with, we have parents to love, and above all we have Jesus to be our Lord.

But sometimes these things aren't quite enough. There are other things which make us sad. *(Show the sad face.)* Perhaps one of our friends has moved away. Perhaps something sad has happened to someone in our family. Or perhaps we don't feel very well. Then we're sad. *(Again demonstrate the sad mask.)*

But then we often do something strange. We don't want people to know we are sad. So we put on a happy mask anyway. *(Place the happy mask in front of the other one.)* We don't want them to see how we feel inside, so we pretend. We cover up our feelings. Maybe we turn on the TV, or go to the ice cream store or perhaps buy a new toy. We hope these things will make us feel better. We hope they will cover up how sad we feel.

That's really too bad, for when we try to cover up our sad feelings we can't be quite honest, and we really can't feel better. We need something else, some other way. The good news is that Jesus knows that, too.

That's why he said that when his children are sad, they

74

can find a different comfort. We don't need to hide our feelings behind something else. *(Demonstrate with mask.)* We know Jesus as the one who comforts us, makes us feel better.

You see, that's really the way to handle our sad feelings. When we feel sad, knowing that Jesus loves us can make us feel better. When we are lonely, we know that Jesus is with us. When things are going wrong, we can remember that God has said that everything works for the good of those who love him. That's the kind of comfort Jesus gives us, to turn sad faces into happy ones. *(Demonstrate.)*

Jesus even came into the world to give it that new kind of happiness. That means we don't have to cover up our feelings or pretend something about them. We can be happy. We have Jesus, and he is Lord of our feelings, too. *(Place the smiling mask over your face.)*

Blessed Are the Aggressive?

SCRIPTURE

Blessed are the meek, for they shall inherit the earth.

Matthew 5:5

PREPARATION

Since this is an action message there will be no preparation necessary other than prompting one boy to push his way to the front of the group. *(If you do not have the children assemble for this part of the worship, you can have him push his way into the front row of the church just as you are ready to start.)*

This morning I really want all of you to be able to see what we're doing. So will you please find a place so you can see. *(This should be the cue for the boy you have prompted to push his way to the front.)* Why Mark, what are you doing? *(Allow Mark to answer. You may have prompted him to say, "Well, I want to see." If he is able to carry this out naturally, so much the better.)*

But Mark, do you think that was the right thing to do? You pushed all the smaller children aside just so you could come to the front. *(Again permit Mark to answer. Develop the conversation in terms of Mark's desire to be in the front row, to be "number one".)*

(Addressing the other children.) Now, didn't you think it was rather strange when Mark pushed his way to the front like that? That's not like Mark at all. He's a very polite and courteous young man. But this morning before anyone came up, I had asked Mark to help me. I asked him to push his way up to the front, just to show everyone how we often act.

Of course we don't do it in church, but there are times we're really like that. We push our way to the front, without even caring how many people we push aside or what we do to them. We like to be "number one" and that means we have to be aggressive. If people aren't, they get left behind.

But Jesus had another way of living, and he had another kind of life for his people too. Jesus said it was more a blessing to be meek, than aggressive. Jesus meant we should be loving and kind and humble with each other. Instead of pushing others aside, Jesus calls us to help others and to share with them.

Of course, that's not the way we are. Naturally we all like to be winners, the number one people, the aggressive ones. But that's the old way of living and we don't have to live that way any more. We are the children of God and we have been baptized into a new life. Jesus takes away our sins of pushing others aside and gives us a new life like his. His life was for other people instead of against them.

That's the way Jesus came to the world. He didn't push anyone aside to try to get to the top. Instead he reached out to help everyone, especially those who had been pushed aside because of our old life. He went to the cross. He suffered and died to give us a new one.

That's our good news. We don't have to say blessed are the aggressive. We can say blessed are the loving, or as Jesus said, blessed are the meek.

A Mind to Work

SCRIPTURE

So we built the wall; and all the wall was joined together to half its height. For the people had a mind to work.

Nehemiah 4:6

PREPARATION

You will need a large number of children's building blocks, and a table on which the blocks can be placed.

This morning I have a box of building blocks. *(Show it.)* I'm going to ask each of you to take one and then we'll build something on this table. *(Indicate it.)* So will you please take a block. *(Wait till everyone has one.)* Now place it on the table anywhere you want. *(This may take just a short time, but allow the children to place the blocks exactly as they choose.)*

All of us have placed our blocks on the table now, haven't we? Very good. Let's see what we've built. *(Look at it as if examining the results. You may wish to over-emphasize your action, to exaggerate your point.)* Really, it doesn't look like we've built anything, have we? We did put our blocks here, but we didn't build a thing. That's too bad. Do you know why we didn't? It was because everyone did it his own way. We didn't work together.

But the good news is that Jesus came to give us a different way. Instead of insisting on our own way, which is the sin of selfishness or pride or stubbornness, we can work with each other. Jesus came into the world to live and to suffer and to die and to rise again for all of us, to bring us together. He forgot himself to work for us, making us his children who can work with each other. In his forgiveness we can forget ourselves, and help one another.

Let's try it that way now. Will you please each take

another block? *(Wait for the children to do so.)* Now, let's build a wall. We won't put our blocks just where we want to by ourselves, but where we can help each other. Let's start right here. *(Indicate where the first person should place his block.)* Now will *(name a child)* place your block right here? *(Indicate the place, follow the procedure with each of the children until the wall is built.)*

Do you see what happens? We built something because we did it together. That's the way God's people are. Jesus has taken away our sin of thinking of ourselves. He gives us a new power to work with each other. That's what the Bible calls "a mind to work."

Something to Remember

SCRIPTURE

Rejoice, O young man, in your youth, and let your heart cheer you in the days of your youth; walk in the ways of your heart and the sight of your eyes. But know that for all these things God will bring you into judgment.

Ecclesiastes 11:9

PREPARATION

Make paper covers to fit four books. Book one should be entitled "How to Behave;" book two, "Christian Doctrine;" book three, "Interesting Bible Stories;" book four, "Our Sins." In this fourth book insert a title page to read "And God's Forgiveness."

I have some books to look at this morning, books we might use in Sunday school and church. Let's look at them.

Here is the first one. (*Indicate it, showing the title.*) In Sunday school we do learn how God wants his people to live. We call that Christian behavior, something very important for us.

Here's something else we study. Who can tell me what this one is about? (*Ask a child to read the title, then ask someone to explain it. Develop a short dialog with the children.*) That's important, too. We're God's people and we want to know the teachings of his Word.

Here's a third book we might study. (*Use the same process as with the second book.*) We do want to know the great things God has done for us, and Bible stories tell us those great things. They are good to know, too.

But now we come to the most important book of all. (*Show the fourth book, asking a child to read the title.*) That's right, this is a book about our sins. But that's only part of it. If we stop with the title we'd be very sad people. "Our Sins" is only the first part. (*Open the book to show the words "And God's Forgiveness."*) That's right, this book is about our sins and God's forgiveness. We need both pages if our book is going to be worthwhile. And we have both pages, thanks to Jesus.

That's why this is the most important book. This book is important *(show the behavior book)*, but we can't behave like Christians without the power Jesus gives us. This book is important too *(show the Christian doctrine book)* but knowing all the teachings doesn't make us children of God. That's true about this book too. *(Indicate the Bible stories book.)* It's good to know the great things God has done but we still need something more. This book gives that something more, when it shows us our sins and God's forgiveness.

This book about forgiveness is really the book for the people of God. We could almost say that every chapter in it is a chapter that Jesus wrote for us. But he didn't write it the way people write books. He did it by being born just a little child for us. He did it by living on our world with people just like us. He did it with his suffering and his dying. He still writes new pages when we show his word of forgiveness.

And that's something to remember! But do you know something? When we remember all of these things that Jesus has done, when we remember our sins and God's forgiveness, the other books make sense too. They all become something to remember.

Fear or Love?

SCRIPTURE

There is no fear in love, but perfect love casts out fear. For fear has to do with punishment, and he who fears is not perfected in love. We love, because he first loved us.

1 John 4:18-19

PREPARATION

From fairly heavy cardboard make a heart large enough to conceal a child's building block behind it. On the back of the heart construct a little tunnel to hold one block. The tunnel should be open at both ends so that you can insert another block, pushing the first one through. Label the heart with the words MY HEART.

Wrap two children's building blocks of equal size. Label the first one FEAR, the second one LOVE. On the reverse side of the second block, draw a cross and the word LOVE.

By this time I think all of us know what this picture represents. Would anybody like to tell us? *(Display the heart and then wait for a child's response.)* That's right. That's really what hearts do represent. They are to be full of love. *(Demonstrate the block with the word LOVE on the front and insert it in the tunnel behind the heart.)* There, we have just filled our hearts with love.

But sometimes something gets in the way of our love, and our hearts can't be filled with it after all. Sometimes we are too afraid to love. *(Display the block marked FEAR.)* We're afraid someone might not understand us, or that they might take advantage of us. We're afraid they won't love us as much. But, when we are afraid, we can't really love. Fear pushes love out of our hearts. *(Demonstrate with the blocks, inserting the FEAR block and pushing the LOVE block out of the little tunnel.)*

That's really true. It's true with people and it's true with God. If we're afraid of each other, we can't really love each other. If we're afraid of God, we can't even love him. Fear pushes out our love. *(Demonstrate once more.)*

On the other hand, love can push out fear, too. It just has to be a stronger love than we have by ourselves. *(Show the reverse side of the block, displaying the cross.)* It has to be a love like this. That's the perfect love that Jesus brought, and that's the reason he came. He came to bring us God's love. He showed that love when he was born as a little baby at Bethlehem. He lived that love when he was with his disciples and all the people he helped and healed. He suffered and died on the cross because he had such strong love. And he came back from the grave to bring his love to the whole world. *(Display the side of the LOVE block marked with the cross and the word LOVE.)* That's the stronger love that pushes out fear. That's the love he gave us when we were baptized, the love he gives us in his Word and in the sacraments.

That's the good news—we have his love and it pushes out fear. *(Insert the LOVE block in the tunnel, pushing the FEAR block out.)*

A Way to Share

SCRIPTURE

And all who believed were together and had all things in common; and they sold their possessions and goods and distributed them to all, as any had need.

Acts 2:44-45

PREPARATION

You will need three fairly large cookies for this message. *(As the children come forward conceal the cookies behind your back.)*

This morning I need two helpers. Who would like to help me? *(Choose two of the children.)*

Actually, I'm not going to ask anything difficult. In fact I'm going to share something with you. I'm going to give you these cookies. *(Show the cookies.)*

Now, let's see. There are two of you and I have three cookies. That's going to make sharing them a little difficult.

I think we'll do it this way. *(Hand one cookie to one and two cookies to the other.)* Yes, that works out well, doesn't it? We've shared the cookies, and each of you received something.

(Turn to the other children for this next question.) Don't you think that worked out well? I thought it would be hard to do, but it was easy, don't you think? *(Open the dialog with the children at this point. Lead them to express the idea that the sharing wasn't quite fair. You may need to point it out, but you will probably receive a response indicating the division wasn't equal.)*

You really are right. It wasn't fair to give Heidi two cookies and Amy only one. We'll have to try something different. Does anybody know how we might solve our problem? *(Undoubtedly one of the children will suggest that you break a cookie in half. Do so, but break it very*

84

unevenly so that one part is very small and the other is much larger.) That was a good idea. Now we can divide the cookies very fairly, can't we? Let's see how this is. *(Hold up the two pieces of the one cookie, one very large and the small one.)* That's better, isn't it? Or do you still think it's not quite fair? *(Again wait for comments, and proceed on the basis of the comments received.)*

That really says something about us all, doesn't it? Even when we receive things we didn't expect, we like to get our share. We don't want someone else to get more than we do. I wonder if anybody could think of a word for that. *(Allow the children to supply some words, possibly leading them to the idea of selfishness.)* There are many words that describe it, but selfishness does tell it best. We want to have just as much or perhaps even more than others. After all, if we could choose a big piece of the cookies or a little piece, most of us would do the same thing; we'd take the bigger piece. We think of ourselves before we think of others.

That's really not the way God wanted people to be. It's the way we became because we're sinners. Our selfishness shows it. But it also shows something else. It shows how much we need Jesus Christ. He came into the world to take away our sin. He didn't think of himself at all, instead he gave everything, even his life for us. That's another way of saying that he suffered and died that we have his forgiveness.

That's good news for God's people. Our loving, forgiving Jesus is with us, and he gives us a new kind of sharing to do. He gives us a new love in place of our selfishness. It happened first on the cross *(hold your cross in front of the children)* and it happens in us whenever Jesus has his way among us. It's his way to share.

Leftovers for God?

SCRIPTURE

Now concerning the contribution for the saints: as I directed the churches of Galatia, so you also are to do. On the first day of every week, each of you is to put something aside and store it up, as he may prosper, so that contributions need not be made when I come. And when I arrive, I will send those whom you accredit by letter to carry your gift to Jerusalem.

1 Corinthians 16:1-3

PREPARATION

You will need about thirty nickels for this demonstration.

This morning we're going to talk about something we all know. It's something we all use, something we all enjoy having. This is what I mean. *(Display the handful of nickels.)* We're going to talk about how to use these nickels.

There are many ways we might use them. There are so many things we need. Let's think of some. *(You may wish to involve children's responses instead of the following. The pattern will be the same, though.)* Perhaps we want to go to the show and that will take ten. *(Set ten nickels aside.)* Then a box of popcorn will be five more, but we have plenty so we'll get one. *(Set five more nickels aside.)* Maybe we'd like a candy bar, and that takes two more. *(Repeat the process setting two more nickels aside.)* And when we come home with our friends we might want to have a coke at the store. *(Set three more nickels aside.)* We need some notebook paper, and that takes five more. *(Set those aside.)* An ice cream bar tastes good after lunch, especially when everybody else has one, and that's another two nickels. *(Place those with the others.)* Now add a pack of chewing gum, and that's another nickel, a couple pieces of bubble gum takes another. *(Set those aside.)*

Oh, we almost forgot. We want to have some for church too. It's a good thing we have a nickel left. We'll put that in church. That nickel is for God's work. Isn't that great? We have everything we wanted and we even had something left over for God. *(Nod your head as if you approved of the idea.)*

But it isn't really so great after all. The idea of giving God leftovers isn't a good idea. God even tells us in his word that we should remember him first. That means we start with him, and we won't be guilty of giving him leftovers.

Let's try that. We have thirty nickels and ten percent of that would be three. We'll set that aside first. *(Set those three aside on a different stack.)* Now let's take out the ten for the show, and the five for the popcorn. *(Do so, continuing with the items you mentioned before.)* Well, there we are. The nickels are all gone. The only thing we didn't get was our gum, but everything else we have.

In fact, the stack for us is very large anyway. It's still a lot bigger than the stack that goes for God's work. *(Indicate the two sizes.)* But this time at least we did it the right way. We didn't give God leftovers. We gave him the first part.

Sometimes that's hard to do, at least we think it is. We do think of ourselves first. That's why we need the power that Jesus gives us. He thought of us first, and came into our world to give himself to us. It's his power which changes us. His forgiveness takes away our sins of thinking of ourselves first and giving God the leftovers. Jesus turns us around, gives us a new direction, a direction in which we remember God first. That's the way for God's people to live, with the power of Jesus Christ. We can give God his part first instead of giving him the leftovers.

Those Other Gods

SCRIPTURE

You shall have no other gods before me. You shall not make for yourself a graven image, or any likeness of anything that is in heaven above, or that is in the earth beneath, or that is in the water under the earth; you shall not bow down to them or serve them; for I the Lord your God am a jealous God, visiting the iniquity of the fathers upon the children to the third and the fourth generation of those who hate me, but showing steadfast love to thousands of those who love me and keep my commandments.

Exodus 20:3-6

PREPARATION

Prepare two collages. The first should have the name of God in the center, and around it various activities of the people of God. These might include children studying in a Sunday school, a Bible, people kneeling at the communion rail, the baptismal font, and so forth. You may choose any pictures you wish to emphasize for this particular part. (A church supply catalog will be a good source for these pictures.)

The second collage should show a group of activities which can interfere with church life. These might be golf clubs, a bicycle, TV, baseball and a bat, a new automobile, water skis, a camper, etc.

This morning we're going to show you two pictures, both of things we like to do. Some of the things we do because we are God's people. Others we do for other reasons. Let's look at the pictures and name the things we see. Maybe you could hold up your hand if you especially like to do some of these things. (Begin with either picture, permitting children to identify what is happening with each scene of the collage, perhaps asking how many like this?)

We were able to name every one of them, weren't we? That's probably because we like to do them all. We like to play ball and to watch TV and to water ski or to go camping. We like to share God's word and to remember that we are baptized people of God and to go to Sunday school and to be in church. They are all good things to do.

Sometimes though, even good things can become a problem. We said these were good things to do, *(indicate the collage of the various sport activities)* but sometimes we get so interested in them that we forget these. *(Indicate the chart of the church activities.)* That means these *(show first collage)* have taken God's place. When our water skiing is more important than our faith it has become a kind of god; or when TV is more important than Sunday school, it takes God's place. When playing golf takes more of our time than hearing the word, it has become a god for us too. Then the good things God has given us have become bad things, because we're using them the wrong way. We give them a place ahead of him. *(Put the activities collage in front of the church collage.)*

But that's not the way God would like us to live. He wants to be God above everything else with all of us. He wants nothing to take his place, so he sent Jesus into the world to take away our sin of putting other things ahead of him. When Jesus came he gave us first place in his life, and because he did we can give first place to him as well.

That doesn't mean these things are bad. *(Indicate the various recreational activities.)* Not at all! Because Jesus came to us to take away our sins, they can be good. We can see them as God's gifts to us, but we know they can't take his place. The people of God can have them both. We have these *(indicate the recreational activities)* as gifts from God, and we have God! *(Indicate that collage.)*

That's My Name

SCRIPTURE

You shall not take the name of the Lord your God in vain, for the Lord will not hold him guiltless who takes his name in vain.

Exodus 20:7

PREPARATION

Prepare half a dozen cardboard name tags, attaching a loop of yarn so they can be placed over the children's heads. If you can, use names of children whom you expect to be present.

This morning again I need six helpers. Let me see, I will choose these. (*Choose the six whose name tags you have prepared in advance. However as the children step forward, place a wrong name tag over each.*) Very good. I have the six helpers and they have their name tags. Now will you please turn so that you can see everyone else and they can see you? Very good!

But, let's see. There is something wrong. Here is Brian, and he has Denise's name tag. Denise's tag tells us that she's Charles, and Charles is really Julie, and everyone is all mixed up. (*Judge the reaction of the children to this. There will probably be some laughing because of it. If not, you might develop the idea that it is rather a humorous mix-up.*)

That's really funny, isn't it? Here we know these people so well and yet we gave them the wrong names. It really is a joke. We know that Brian isn't Denise, and Charles isn't Julie, and so on.

But how do you think Brian would feel if I kept calling him Denise? It's funny right now isn't it, but how do you think he would feel? Brian, how would you feel? (*Develop the idea that he would not like it.*)

We know why Brian wouldn't like it. Our names are very important to us. They tell people who we are. We don't want it given to someone else, or used in the wrong way by someone else. Our names are important to us.

And that's the way it is with God's name too. We can't separate a person from his name. And we can't separate God's name from him. And because he is God, he doesn't want his name used in the wrong way. He doesn't want people to mix it up, to make fun of his name, or to use it in anger. Sadly, we sometimes do just that. But that is not the way God wants his name to be used.

There is another way we can use God's name. When Jesus came into the world he gave us another way. He told us that we could call on God's name when we wanted to pray to him. That's a right way to use God's name. He told us we can use God's name in our praises. Saying "Thank you, God, for all you have done," is another right way. Jesus came to bring God's love to us. He gives us a loving way to use his name. He even suffered and died to take away our sins of mixing up his name, of using his name in fun, or cursing it in anger. We can be the people of God, with the right way to use his name.

A Day to Remember

SCRIPTURE

Remember the Sabbath Day to keep it holy.

Not neglecting to meet together, as is the habit of some, but encouraging one another, and all the more as you see the Day drawing near.

Exodus 20:8 and Hebrews 10:25

PREPARATION

Cut two months from a large calendar. If you do not have a very large calendar available, it would be better to draw out the calendar pages for two months on large sheets of paper. On the Sundays of one page paste pictures of Sunday activities such as mowing the lawn, playing golf, sleeping in, or having a barbeque. Items cut from magazines or catalogs serve to suggest these activities. On the other calendar page place an item of a church activity on each Sunday, a Bible, communion vessels, a group of children in Sunday school, a choir singing, the pastor preaching and so on.

What day is today? *(Wait for the answer.)* You're right, it's Sunday. I wonder if anybody can tell me what makes today a special day? *(Again wait for the answer. It may be a little confusing, since the children will probably try to think first of some major festival. As you converse with them, elicit the idea that every Sunday is a special day.)*

That's right, it's a special day because it's a Sunday. Probably our parents don't have to go to work today. That makes it special. Maybe we've planned a picnic for this afternoon or a barbecue for this evening. That makes it special. But above all, we're doing something right now that makes today special. What is that? *(Allow the children to give their answers. Expect such answers as going to church, hearing God's word, and so forth. Make appropriate comments with each one.)*

That's right. Those things make this a special day. They make it God's day in a special way. Today we are sharing him and his word. And they make it our day in a special way, too, because today we're celebrating that we are together as God's people.

But sometimes people have funny reasons for calling this a special day. Let's look at this calendar. *(Show the one with the non-church activities.)* For some people today is a special day because of things they can do. *(Point to the various activities and ask the children to identify them.)* For them that makes this day a special day. Sadly, that's not really very special. We can do those things on any day.

So, let's look at this other calendar. *(Show the other page.)* This is a special calendar giving reasons why God's people know this is a special day. *(Again invite the children to identify and comment on each one of the activities.)* Right, today is the day we can do all of these things. Oh, certainly we can study God's word every day, and that would make any day a special day. Certainly we can sing songs to him any day and that makes any day a special day too. But today is the day we can come together to do that. Today we remember him especially.

It's a special day for another reason, too. It's the day that God's people remember Jesus' resurrection from the grave. When the people of God first were coming together to worship, they decided to worship on Sundays. That would remind them of Easter, so every day we come together like this, we are celebrating a little Easter.

That really makes it special. Jesus came out of the grave and into all of the world to give us a special day to remember, just the way we're doing right now.

To Be Continued

SCRIPTURE

But as for you, continue in what you have learned and have firmly believed, knowing from whom you learned it and how from childhood you have been acquainted with the sacred writings which are able to instruct you for salvation through faith in Christ Jesus. All scripture is inspired by God and profitable for teaching, for reproof, for correction, and for training in righteousness, that the man of God may be complete, equipped for every good work.

2 Timothy 3:14-17

PREPARATION

Prepare three imitation certificates, possibly by rolling white paper into a scroll and tying with a gold ribbon. The use of a gold notary seal as is used in church certificates will give a more official appearance on the certificate.

Certificate number one should read: This certifies that Timmy Christian has finished his study of the Bible.

Certificate number two should say: This certifies that Timmy Christian knows everything about the word of God.

Certificate number three should read: This certifies that Timmy Christian has completed this year's work and has much more to study.

On the third certificate in large print add the words TO BE CONTINUED.

(NOTE: This particular message is suitable for confirmation day, rally day, or the ending of an educational term.)

When a person finishes school he gets a special paper. It's called a diploma, a sign that he has completed his classes.

I have three diplomas this morning. Two of them show the ideas we sometimes have about our studies as God's children. The third one tells us something else. So let's look at them, and see which one fits us.

Who would like to unroll this and read it for us? *(Give the scroll to one of the children, waiting while he unrolls and reads it.)* That is a sort of diploma, isn't it? It tells us we have completed everything, and there is nothing more to do. We know everything there is to know! Sadly that's the way some people feel when they finish their Sunday school or their instruction classes. They feel they should get a diploma that says they never have to study again.

Now, let's look at this one. *(Again allow a child to open it and read it, commenting in the same way as you did with the first.)*

But now here is a third diploma which is much different. Who would like to read that one for us? *(Again, choose a child to do so.)* What a difference that was, especially with those three very important words. Tom, will you hold the diploma so that we can all see it once more?

Now, let's see, which three words do we think are those important ones? *(Wait for the children to respond.)* That's right. The words TO BE CONTINUED. They mean our study is to go on. They mean our learning about Jesus isn't going to stop and our sharing his word isn't finished. It will go on; it's to be continued.

There are several good reasons for this diploma. One is that we can never learn everything about Jesus. We could study until the day that we are one hundred five years old and not know everything about him and his word. So it's good to continue.

That's a good reason, but there is a better one. The better reason is that Jesus' love is always continuing for us. He never finishes caring for us, he never stops his forgiveness to us. He has always continued his presence with us. That means every time we share his word or come to the sacrament we are continuing with him. That's the way God's people grow. Our studies, our sharing, our life with Jesus don't come to an end. They're something to be continued.

A Faith that Grows

SCRIPTURE

Like newborn babes, long for the pure spiritual milk, that by it you may grow up to salvation.

1 Peter 2:2

PREPARATION

Prepare a set of flash cards showing the stock figure of a boy. The cards should be identical, with the boy the same size on all. *(You may wish to mark the back of the cards with the number two, the second card with five, the third card with number ten, the fourth with number twelve, to make your presentation easier.)*

Also prepare a second set of our cards beginning with a stick figure the same size as Tommy at age two. Increase the size of the figure with each card.

This morning I want to show you a picture of a little boy. We'll say his name is Tommy, although it really doesn't make any difference what his name is. We're just going to look at his picture for a little while. Here is a picture of Tommy at age two *(show the picture)*, and here is Tommy at age five. *(Show that picture.)* This is Tommy when he was ten years old, and this when he was twelve. *(Show both pictures.)* Now I wonder if you notice something funny about these pictures? *(Wait for the children to comment. Be assured that someone will notice that they are all the same size. If that comment is not forthcoming, lead the children to see it.)*

That's right, and that is different, isn't it? We would expect a person to be larger at age twelve than he had been at age two. If he wasn't we'd hurry to get a doctor to find out why, and we'd ask the doctor for medicine or something to help him grow.

Of course, the same thing is true about God's children too. Just as we get bigger and stronger and taller in our bodies, God wants us to grow stronger and taller in our faith too. He wants us to grow in the things we know about Jesus and how much we believe in him. It would really be sad if we'd just be the same size Christians when we're two or five or ten or twelve. *(Show the pictures once again.)*

And we have the way to grow in our faith. We don't even have to go to a doctor for it. We have Jesus. He said, "I am the way and the truth and the life" and he shared his love and his word with us. When he was with his disciples he took a piece of bread and he said "This is my body" and a cup of wine and said "This is my blood." He shares that sacrament with us too. These are his ways for us to grow in our faith.

We're baptized, and we're like this. *(Show first card of second set.)* Then as we hear Jesus' word, we grow. *(Show second card.)* We learn of him and grow some more. *(Show third card.)* We have the sacrament and grow more. *(Show last card.)* We don't have to stay the same size.

Our Upside-down World

Now the works of the flesh are plain: immorality, impurity, licentiousness, idolatry, sorcery, enmity, strife, jealousy, anger, selfishness, dissension, party spirit, envy, drunkenness, carousing, and the like. I warn you, as I warned you before, that those who do such things shall not inherit the kingdom of God. But the fruit of the Spirit is love, joy, peace, patience, kindness, goodness, faithfulness, gentleness, self-control; against such there is no law.

Galatians 5:19-23

PREPARATION

From light cardboard cut six small cards, approximately one inch by two inches. Print the following words ANGER, FEAR, ENVY, JEALOUSY, QUARRELING, HATRED, on separate cards. On the reverse of each card print one of the following words: LOVE, FAITH, GENTLENESS, GOODNESS, PEACE, JOY. *(Print the one set of words upside down. It will become obvious as the lesson progresses why this is a necessity.)*

Attach the words to a map of the world in such a way that when the map is held upside down the words describing our sins will be showing. When the map is right side up, the cards should fall the other way and the Christian virtues should appear. *(This will require a little experimentation. You may find it necessary to tape a small washer or weight at the bottom of each card so it will hinge easily.)*

All of you know what this is, don't you? That's right, it's a map of the world. *(Hold the map upside down, with the sin words showing.)* But do you notice something about it? There's something wrong with it. Who can tell me what it is? *(Invite the children to comment.)* That's right. It's upside down. But you'll notice that even with the map upside down there are some things we can see about the world. We can see the problems people have, and the way we often live.

(Invite the children to share the words which are showing. You may wish to make a short comment about the anger or fear or hatred, etc. which is in the world.) That

98

is sad news, the bad situation of our world. It has things all upside down, and people live with these sins. They even think that's the natural way to live.

But that's why Jesus came into the world. He turned it right side up again. *(Demonstrate with the map, turning it right side up.)* And did you notice when he turned the world right side up, the sins changed. *(Indicate the cards.)* Now instead of anger we have love, instead of fear we have faith. *(Continued with the various virtues listed.)*

That's the good news for God's people. We don't have to live in an upside down world any longer. We live with Jesus, who came into our world, and who suffered and died to turn it right side up. He did it with his cross. *(As you talk about the upside down world and the right side up world, emphasize your words by turning the map.)* And when he suffered and died on the cross he gave us a right side up way.

That's our good news. Jesus is living in us so that we can live right side up. When we were baptized, he turned us the right way around. With his word he still shares right side up living with us. He gives us a right side up way for an upside down world.

God Knows!

SCRIPTURE

Are not two sparrows sold for a penny? And not one of them will fall to the ground without your Father's will. But even the hairs of your head are all numbered. Fear not, therefore; you are of more value than many sparrows.

Matthew 10:29-31

PREPARATION

Since this is an action response no preparation will be necessary.

(11-12-78)

This morning I'd like you to play a little counting game with me. I think most of you know what counting games are. You probably have them in school, when you study mathematics.

We're going to have a very simple counting game. Let's start by asking how many eyes we have? *(Wait for the answer.)* That's right. How many ears? *(Again wait for the answer, commenting about how simple the question was.)* Let's try something a little harder. How many fingers do you have? *(Wait for the answer.)* Right, there were a few more this time, weren't there? How many toes do you have? Well, all of us know that too. There is no problem in counting eyes or ears or fingers or toes or anything like that. We know those things.

Now let's see if we can answer a harder question. How many hairs are there on your head? *(Wait for an answer.)* That's a little harder, isn't it? In fact, it's a lot harder. We have to agree we don't know that answer. Not a person here knows how many hairs are on his head. No one in the whole world knows.

That's not quite true. God knows! And he is with us in the world. He knows how many eyes and ears and fingers and toes we all have; he gave them to us. He even knows how many hairs there are on our heads.

100

That's something good for us, to know that God knows. Our God who knows so much about us he even knows things we don't even know about ourselves. That's why Jesus could tell people not to be afraid of anything because God knows all about us. He knows everything you need. God even knows that little tiny thing about how many hairs there are on your head.

Sometimes we forget that God knows. Sometimes we get worried about things that might happen. We get all upset when it seems things are going wrong for us. But Jesus is with us, and there is no reason to be worried, no reason to get upset. God knows all about it.

That's the good news God's people always have. Sometimes we might have troubles, but God knows what we need. Sometimes we might be sick or have an accident, but God knows what will be the best for us. He sent Jesus to remind us that he knows everything about us, even when we forget him. He sent Jesus to show how much he loves us. He even sent Jesus to take away our sin of forgetting, just so we can remember that God knows.

When Someone Is Wrong

SCRIPTURE

If your brother sins against you, go and tell him his fault, between you and him alone. If he listens to you, you have gained your brother.

Matthew 18:15

PREPARATION

Prepare a set of pictures using stick figure drawings.

Picture one should show one person talking to another. Pictures two through six should show people whispering into the ear of other people, showing different poses so that obviously they are different people. Picture seven should be one person speaking to a large group of people.

This morning we're going to talk about something very difficult. We're going to talk about getting along with each other, when someone has hurt us. That does happen, doesn't it? It happens that someone hurts our feelings or does something we don't like or does something we think is wrong. So this morning we want to talk about how God's people act when that happens.

God did tell us a way. Here is a picture of that way. *(Show picture number one and ask the children to comment, drawing from them the idea of one person talking to another.)* That's exactly it. That's the thing God told us to do. He said we are to tell that person, and no one else. Then we can get it straightened out.

But sadly, that's not the way we usually do. These pictures show what we usually do. *(Show pictures two through six, again drawing comments from the children about each one.)* That's right. We say to our friends, "Hey, did you hear about this?" or "Did you know what Susie did?" or "Wait til I tell you what Timmy did to me!"

It doesn't seem like so much when we're telling just one person at a time, but here's what it really amounts to. *(Show the last picture of one person addressing a large group.)* It really means that we are passing on bad news about someone else. The sad part is that it hurts the other person, and it hurts us too, for we don't get the problem taken care of. It might make us feel very important or very right, but it can't settle our problems.

But Jesus knew that such a way of handling things would only cause great problems for his people. It would only lead to problems between them, like fences which separate them. *(Hold the cards so that they form a barrier between you and the children.)* That's why Jesus came. He came into the world to say living that way is not a good way to live. Living with forgiveness is better. Living with anger is not the right way, living with love is. Gossiping and telling others about our friend's sins is nothing good; helping one another is. So Jesus came into the world to bring us his love, to bring us his forgiveness to give his life for us as his way of helping us.

And that's the good news. He has made us into a new kind of people, the kind of people who can be helpers to each other, who can love each other and who can talk with one another. We have been baptized *(if the font is near, point to it)* into a new life with each other. Jesus gives himself to us so that we can live it.

That means we do have a way to handle it when someone does something wrong. We have the way of love and forgiveness. And then, do you know something? Sharing them makes the hurt go away, and we can think of each other as people we love instead of as someone who might have done something wrong. That's why we share with each other. *(Show card number one.)*

Light for the Darkness

SCRIPTURE

In the beginning was the Word, and the Word was with God, and the Word was God. He was in the beginning with God; all things were made through him, and without him was not anything made that was made. In him was life, and the life was the light of men. The light shines in the darkness, and the darkness has not overcome it.

There was a man sent from God, whose name was John. He came for testimony, to bear witness to the light, that all might believe through him. He was not the light, but came to bear witness to the light.

The true light that enlightens every man was coming into the world.

John 1:1-9

PREPARATION

Cover the interior of a shoebox with black construction paper. On one inside end of the box draw a white cross inside a white heart. Use only the outline for the heart. Cut a hole in the bottom of the box to fit the lens of a flashlight.

On the end of the box opposite the cross and heart cut an opening through which a child might look. (Note: It is very important that no light gets into the box through this opening. You may find it desirable to make another cylinder of black construction paper to insert into the box so the child looks through the cylinder into the box, lessening the possibility that light might enter the box.)

The cover should also be lined with black paper and fastened securely to the box.

This morning I'm going to need someone to help me again. I need someone to tell me what he sees inside this box. (*Choose a child and have him look into the box with the flashlight turned off.*) All right, Greg, please tell us what you saw. (*Wait for him to answer and draw the response that he saw absolutely nothing.*) That's right. You couldn't see anything in the box, could you? It's hard to see in the dark, and when a box is as dark as this one is inside, it's impossible to see.

Greg, let's try it again. (*Turn on the flashlight.*) All

right Greg, what did you see this time? Very good. You saw a heart and a cross. Well, why did you see them this time when you didn't see them last time? *(Wait for his answer, and engage in a short dialog with him about it.)*

That's it, you could see this time because the box was light. You couldn't the last time because it had been all dark. You could see the heart and the cross because of the light in the box.

You see, that's exactly the way our world was too God tells us that it was like living in darkness. People really didn't know what love was. They couldn't see the heart because of the darkness and they couldn't see forgiveness, either. People lived in the darkness we call sin, and that's the way the world would have gone on living.

But that's not the way God wanted his world to live. He had made the world, but it had decided to live in its darkness. Still God sent his son to bring it back into the light. He sent Jesus to be the light of the world. *(Turn on the flashlight once more.)* Just as we can all look into this box right now *(hold it in front of several of the children so they can see)* to see God's love and his cross because the box is filled with light, so we can find God's love and his forgiveness in Jesus. He is the light of the world.

That just leaves us one question, would we rather live in darkness or in the light?

God even has his answer for that. He made us the children of light he says, when we were baptized. He brought the bright beams of his love to us in Jesus Christ. We can live in light because Jesus is the light of the world.

The Hammer on the Rock

SCRIPTURE

Let the prophet who has a dream tell the dream, but let him who has my word speak my word faithfully. What has straw in common with wheat? says the Lord. Is not my word like fire, says the Lord, and like a hammer which breaks a rock in pieces?

Jeremiah 23:28-29

PREPARATION

For this message you will need a hammer and a broken piece of cement or cinder block. (You may wish to experiment before your presentation to decide if you really do want to break the block. You can 'fake it' by taping pieces of the block together so that they break apart easily with a light blow. It is more effective, though, if you actually break the block.)

Who knows what I have here? (*Demonstrate your articles, showing the hammer first, and then the block.*) What did you say? What is this? (*Show the piece of block. Allow the children to give various answers. You will probably receive several.*) I'm sorry, but you are wrong. I'll tell you why in just a little while.

Maybe you can tell me what this is. (*Show the hammer. Again wait for the answers.*) Most of you say this is a hammer. I'll just have to say wrong again. Now I'll tell you what these are.

This rock is a person, just like you are and just like I am. I mean, this is a pretend person, and you'll know why very soon, after I tell you about this. (*Show the hammer.*)

This is the Word of God. That's right. God said his word is a hammer. Really, he said that it's like a hammer, hitting on a rock. (*Demonstrate the action.*) So what is this? (*Show the piece of stone, and wait until someone remembers it's supposed to be a person.*) Right; it's a person. And this is God's Word, hitting that person.

(Repeat the action, this time breaking the piece of stone, if possible. If it breaks, register appropriate comment. If it does not, say something like: "Of course, if I hit it harder, it would break, but that would make a big mess in here. So let's just pretend that it breaks.")

What God wants to tell us is that's the way his word comes to us. It comes to smash our sins. But do you know something? We don't always like that. When the word comes with all that force, we sometimes pull away from it. *(Demonstrate by hitting at the rock, but pulling it away before the hammer hits.)* We don't mind if the hammer of the word just chips off a little bit of our sin, or if it just touches us very lightly. *(Demonstrate.)* But we don't like to be broken into pieces by having all our sins shattered.

Yet that's why Jesus came. The Bible even calls him the Word of God in a person, instead of as a hammer. But he came to show us our sins, so that we could become his new people in his forgiveness. He comes to us in his word now and in the sacrament to rebuild us. *(Using the pieces of rock, place them together in a new and taller formation.)* That's the Good News God's people have. The Son of God let himself be hammered to a cross and then sealed in a grave. But he came out of it. He hammered our sins away, and puts us together as new people without them. We don't have to duck away from his word; his hammer won't hurt us. It will rebuild us.

Ready to Be Filled

SCRIPTURE

And do not grieve the Holy Spirit of God, in whom you were sealed for the day of redemption. Let all bitterness and wrath and anger and clamor and slander be put away from you, will all malice, and be kind to one another, tenderhearted, forgiving one another, as God in Christ forgave you.

Ephesians 4:30-32

PREPARATION

You will need a small table for this message. On it place three clear glass water tumblers, each containing water in which a different food coloring has been mixed. (Use vivid colors, since the lighter shades cannot be seen from any distance. Easter egg dyes work very well, although there may be some problem in cleaning.)

Label three cups as follows:

Cup number one: Label LOVE on the one side. Then turn the cup over, and label the other side HATRED, so that the words will read LOVE when the cup is right side up, HATRED when it is upside down.

Cup number two: Label in the same way, using the words KINDNESS and BITTERNESS.

Cup number three: Label in the same way, with the words FORGIVENESS and ANGER.

Also, label the three glasses of liquid: Love, Kindness, Forgiveness.

This morning we're going to hear about something God does for each of us when he fills us with his Holy Spirit. We're going to ask you to pretend that you're like these cups. (*Indicate them.*) How about that? Did you ever think you'd be a teacup?

Of course not. And you're really not a teacup; you're a person. But you're a person to be filled with something, to be filled with God's gifts for us. One of these is LOVE. (*Take the liquid container marked LOVE, and indicate that you are going to pour it into the cup. But before you begin pouring, turn the cup upside down, turning it so that the word HATRED shows.*)

Now that's something, isn't it? What would happen if I'd pour this love *(indicate the glass)* into this upside-down cup? *(Allow the children to answer.)* Would this cup *(indicate it)* have any of this love in it? *(Again wait for the answer.)* You're right; it wouldn't have any of it. Our cup is turned over. *(Repeat the process with each of the others.)*

But do you know, we're just like these teacups, when they're upside down. We get angry with each other; we are bitter with one another; we sometimes don't even want to forgive each other. God wants to pour his love into us and his kindness into us and his forgiveness into us, and we still like to keep our cups turned upside down.

But do you know something, our God is so loving and kind and forgiving toward us that he wants us to have a better kind of life than one which is filled with bad feelings. That's why he sent Jesus into the world. Jesus came to turn our cups right side up again with his love and his forgiveness. He was so kind to us that he even let people put him on a cross where they crucified him. That's the way he took away our sins. They even thought they had sealed him in a grave. *(Indicate such an action by turning a cup upside down for emphasis.)* But he didn't stay in the grave. He came out. *(Again, act this out with one of the cups.)* And he is with us right now, turning our cups right side up, to fill them with himself. *(Begin pouring the various liquids into the cups.)*

So we can be new people, filled up with his love, filled up with his kindness, filled with his forgiveness. Of course, if this overflowed, *(indicate the liquid)* it might ruin this table or the floor. But when Jesus' love overflows it doesn't ruin anything. Things are ruined only if we are stubborn, and keep our cups upside down. But Jesus turns us right side up, making us ready to be filled.

Our Choice of Checks

One of the multitude said to him, "Teacher, bid my brother divide the inheritance with me." But he said to him, "Man, who made me a judge or divider over you?" And he said to them, "Take heed, and beware of all covetousness; for a man's life does not consist in the abundance of his possessions." And he told them a parable, saying, "The land of a rich man brought forth plentifully; and he thought to himself, 'What shall I do, for I have nowhere to store my crops?' And he said, 'I will do this; I will pull down my barns, and build larger ones; and there I will store all my grain and my goods. And I will say to my soul, Soul, you have ample goods laid up for many years; take your ease, eat, drink, be merry.' But God said to him, 'Fool! This night your soul is required of you; and the things you have prepared, whose will they be?' So is he who lays up treasure for himself, and is not rich toward God."

Luke 12:13-21

PREPARATION

If you have some large size bank checks available such as are used in commercial accounts, use four of them. Otherwise you may wish to make large checks, so that they can be seen and read easily. Make them out as follows:

Date: The date you use this material.

Payable to: If you can fill in names of three of the young people, do so. Otherwise leave this space blank, and hand out the checks to any of the children you choose.

Amount:

Check number one: Ten dollars.

Check number two: One new ten-speed bicycle.

Check number three: Your own color TV for your room.

Check number four should be made out as follows:
Date: Every day.
Payable to: All God's people.
Amount: All my love, always.

If you wish, the signature on the first three checks can read "Your Father." On the last one, have it read "Your Heavenly Father."

I think all of you know what I have in my hand. *(Show the checks.)* That's right. They are checks, just like the paycheck many of us get, and many of your parents or brothers and sisters get. But these are different. They are for different things.

Now, who would like this one? It's for ten dollars. *(Act out the process of picking a child. Repeat the process with each check, going up in value as you do.)* Wow, think of that. We thought the check for ten dollars was great, but look at this one for a new bicycle. Who would want that one? *(Again, pick someone.)* Here's another one, for even more. This is for a color TV. Who would want that? All of these things are really great, aren't they? Who got the best one? *(Permit the children to respond, developing the idea that perhaps your dividing them wasn't done fairly, perhaps even suggesting a little anger because of it.)*

But now, let's look at this check. *(Show at least one.)* That's really something different, isn't it? And look, it's for every one of us. And not only that, let's see how long it will last. *(Indicate the words "for always," and invite one of the children to read them.)*

Sadly, though, sometimes we get so excited about these other checks *(take them back from the children)* that we forget all about this one. *(Indicate the check with "All my love".)* We put these in front, and this one gets pushed to the back. *(Place the other checks in front, hiding the one from the heavenly Father.)* We even argue and quarrel about how much we get, or how much others get, and if we think they got more. We make the wrong choices about our checks.

That's why Jesus came into the world, though. He came to set our choices right again, by making his own right choices for us. He chose to suffer and die for everyone of us, almost as if he were going to write out a check for our forgiveness. That's really what he did for us when we were baptized. That's what he does for us when we share his word. That's what he's doing for us when we receive him in the sacrament. He's putting things in the right order again for us, with his love in front. *(Indicate this with your actions.)*

And that even means we can enjoy all these other things, too. When we have this check *(show the check of the Father's love)* we can recognize everything as his gift to us as well. That's Good News, and it means the right choice of checks.